CITIZEN Mitten

CITIZEN Mitten

My life with a cat my family says was as nutty as me

William Voedisch

East Wind Ink
Marine-on-St. Croix, Minnesota

Publisher:
East Wind Ink
www.citizenmitten.com

Photographs by the author
Editor: Patricia Morris

Publisher's Cataloging-in-Publication Data available upon request
Library of Congress Control Number: 2009905042

First edition
13 12 11 10 01 02 03 04

ISBN 978-0-9823809-0-1

for Jon

This book is dedicated to
Laurie, Rob and Amy
who, for nearly 20 years,
endured their own *Calvin and Hobbes* . . .
me and the Mitten.

Contents

A note from Mitten

Yes, another pet book.

"A cat version of *Marley and Me?*" you might be saying to yourself as you browse this. "Ho hum."

I'm Mitten. Well, the spirit of Mitten, anyway. Having left this life on December 8, 2000, I have been haunting my owner ever since, bugging him to write my story, and he finally got around to doing it. It's about time, Billy. So what's wrong with a cat getting a little ink?

Billy has not read *Marley and Me*, even though a copy is around the house someplace. Actually, he didn't want to be influenced by the runaway bestseller, so he has avoided it. But my thought might be this: *Citizen Mitten* is perhaps no more a "cat" version of *Marley and Me* than I was a cat version of John Grogan's beloved dog, Marley. I don't know about Marley, but I was just so weird and unpredictable compared to all the other cats Billy has known in his 64 years, that he just felt compelled to share my story, and how I nearly drove the whole family crazy. But a cat is just so unlike a dog in so many ways that the two books just have to be different. Anyway, as cats go, I guess I was more than just a little nuts, and that's probably why the nutty Billy and I bonded so closely.

Another difference is that Mr. Grogan is a professional writer, a journalist, and those skills surely helped him as he told his story of Marley. My Billy is just a guy who had a special cat (that would be moi) and wanted to share my craziness through his first serious attempt at creative writing.

For sure, I was his cat of a lifetime. I passed away after a life of 19 years and 8 months. That's Billy and Laurie's estimate of my age, anyway, since I belonged to someone else and found them when I was perhaps six months old. It's all a little fuzzy, but I recall being abandoned.

My ability to find trouble was already well developed in 1981 when I wormed my way into their lives. Knowing my adventurous spirit early on, they had plenty of opportunity to find me another home or take me to an animal shelter, hopefully for adoption. Somehow, those options just never crossed their minds.

So it's been eight years since I left this life and here he goes, finally trying to do justice to me, the little goof who stole his heart, and perhaps some of his wife's jewelry.

I must tell you, however, that this book is not all me, all the time (gee, why not?). Other cats and dogs share some of the ink. Then there are episodes where family and friends snuck in, but they link back to me in some fashion, however convoluted.

I was a funny cat and so this is mostly a funny book, assuming Billy's writing has done me justice, and I think it has. It's also quite sad in spots. Because they love their pets so, when one of us is sick or dying, they are crushed. There is a chapter that goes into some detail about oncology and dogs. It was very hard for Billy to write as it deals with the very tragic loss of their first golden retriever, Kirby. It was even hard for me to read. We cats are fortunate because cancer is a dog thing right now. If you have a dog, you will want to read the chapter, "Dying without dignity."

You dog lovers, who may have little time for us cats, will find some fun stories about dogs. Billy called upon my spirit and his memories of me for inspiration and guidance, so I kinda like to think of us as co-authors. One of our mutual goals is that, after reading *Citizen Mitten,* you dog lovers might find yourself with a better appreciation for us cats. We can be truly hilarious.

Today, Billy and Laurie have five cats and two dogs to keep them occupied, plus farm critters, two wonderful adult children and their significant others, and a lot of retirement activities . . . but no Mitten. Billy misses me even now.

Who can blame him?

Acknowledgments

I could never have done this book alone. Having zero creative writing experience, and knowing maybe less than zero about getting this thing off the ground, I consulted with a few people I trust, and they were all in agreement on one important point: "Get professional help." I hope they were talking about the book and not my mental condition.

Everyone said editing your own writing never works. When working on my own, the more I read the drafts, the worse I got at finding errors. Plus I knew it needed some structural rework. I started with the only person I knew who lived this stuff, son Rob. A writer who also teaches creative writing, Rob saw the book in its early stages and recommended some structural and stylistic changes to the early chapters that worked so very well to make this a much more interesting effort. Thank you, son.

OK, never be your own editor. Perhaps this one is just as true: a family member as your editor can be a tough way to go. Rob eventually found that being editor to dear old dad's work was pretty difficult to do, and we mutually decided he would step back, as I went on the hunt for a professional editor.

My thanks to good friend "Dot" Molstad, a great mom to shelties and cats, well-versed in the business of writing, editing and publishing, for referring me to my editor, Patricia Morris of St. Paul. Patricia has been extremely helpful showing me what I forgot . . . as if I ever knew . . . about good writing style, proper word use, and insights into apparently her best friend, the *comma*. Besides finding a ton of errors, she would wring more of the story out of me with the occasional "OK, now, is that all there is?" Pat Morris is a true professional who really made all the difference in this project.

Dot will be helping with some marketing ideas in case I think someone besides family and tolerant friends might want to read this thing.

Of course, these helpful ladies should both realize that, besides a few copies to the obvious victims, the only mass-marketing of this might be at my funeral, where all attendees will get a copy, perhaps signed on my death bed. "One per household, please."

A big *thank you* goes to spousal unit Laurie, who helped migrate me through some of the computer crapola required to deal with the largest document I've ever created. She was just a champ and so understanding. Mitten passed away before digital photography reached this household, so there was some organizing of original pictures, which fell to me. But as the official family photographer, Laurie supplied all of the digital photos for the more recent stuff. She also did a proofreading for errors and fact checking. Thanks, Junior.

My eternal appreciation goes to the kids, Rob and Amy, for putting up with the Mighty Mitten all those years.

A final thank you to Rob for making me realize that creative writing is *hard work,* something he had been saying for years but which I now fully appreciate. It was his passion for writing that sort of got me started on this project. Watching Rob, I realized that the process of creative writing can be such a positive thing for any writer, not just the commercially successful ones.

Our heart felt appreciation to Brad and Cody, two neighborhood kids who have so reliably done "barn chores" for us for so many years, and who have taken care of our animals, large and small, when needed. Also, a special nod to Laurie's brother, Rick, who has "farm sat" the whole works, taking care of our many animals, mowing grass and plowing snow, while Laurie and I have taken the occasional trip together.

And finally, thanks to the Mitten, for finding me and bringing such nuttiness and joy to my life, especially at a time when I really needed a friend and some serious cheering up. And of course, I must acknowledge the little gremlin for being the spark of inspiration for this book.

Mitten, you were the best kitty ever . . . *if only to me.*

Foreword

This book is as much about Bill as about his pets, and that's not such a bad thing. The picture of Bill that comes through in the reading adds to the drama of the tales, and leads one to glimpse and appreciate a facet or two of the thinking of a pretty darned decent man.

I've known Bill and Laurie many years. My first encounter with Laurie was shortly after I opened my practice twenty years ago. She said she had several animals and had stopped in simply to welcome me to the community. Her welcome was pleasant and professional and since that time she has become one of my most appreciated clients.

Bill didn't show up at the clinic during those early visits by Laurie. But when he eventually rolled in, with a few days of stubble, work boots, grubby trousers, work shirt and cap, my first thought was "Where did Laurie find this vagrant?"

I have come to know Bill much better and the fact that he and Laurie are a couple doesn't seem quite as incongruent as it once did. Bill is retired, farms, is active in the community and doesn't put on airs. He is a positive and upbeat man.

I chose to study veterinary medicine because I wanted to work with animals. In actual fact, the job entails working with people more than animals. Because our relationship is predominantly professional, it is not difficult for me to state what has endeared Bill and Laurie to me over the years. We meet on a single common ground: they want and expect from me the best possible veterinary care for all of their animals — a veterinarian could ask for nothing more in a client. My greatest wish is that all of my clients would share Bill and Laurie's concern for, and their ability and willingness to care for, all of the animals in their keeping.

A few weeks ago I arrived at my clinic and was greeted by a lady in my reception area.

"What's up?" I asked as I came through the door.

"We need to have him put to sleep," said the lady, nodding toward the black lab next to her. "He's eaten a rock."

"How do you know he's eaten a rock?" I asked.

"He's been vomiting for two days and he's been operated on twice before for eating a rock," she said. "Once it was $400 and the next time it was $800."

I thought she was probably right about the diagnosis. Dogs have a way of swallowing things they shouldn't swallow and many of these dogs are repeat offenders.

"Well, I don't want to kill your dog,"

Sadly she offered, "But I can't afford the surgery again."

"Then I'll do it for nothing," I said. "Just leave him with us and we'll find time today to take the rock out."

My assistant took the dog to the kennel and I told the lady I'd see her later that afternoon. An x-ray confirmed the presence of a rock in the dog's small intestine.   We took the rock out without any trouble — it was a simple surgery — and the dog is doing fine today. The owner of the dog paid me what she could for the surgery.

If it wasn't for clients like Bill and Laurie, I wouldn't be able to do such things for people and their pets. I appreciate these two people more than you can possibly imagine.

Bill's book contains a lot of goodness, a little sadness and some triumphs in its pages. You'll enjoy the read as much as I did.

Steven Frech, DVM
Scandia, Minnesota

Cast of Characters

To help our therapy horseback riding non-profit a few years back, I sold programs at a major equestrian Grand Prix jumping event in Minnesota. My sales pitch went something like this: "Programs! Get your Programs! You can't tell who's falling off without a Program!" I heard somebody say they would find another job for me at next year's show. Hrumpf.

It's not so much a program but you might find this cast of characters helpful. Alternate names are listed in parentheses.

Four-legged characters:

Bailey   (Baby Bails, Young Man, Youngster of Men, Young, B-O-Y, B)
Our current male golden; he is the teddy bear of all time.

Brownie
One of Katie's two puppies. This one had a brown tummy.

Buttons   (Needles)
Our first cat when we were kids. Dad's cat of a lifetime.

Callie (Callie Kitty, Barn Mitten, Barn Naoz)
Our current barn cat. She's an excellent mouser and looks the part; a real "lunch box."

Dexter (Baby Dex)
Female littermate to Katie; puppy to MC.

Earl (Earl Gray)
Recently graduated from the barn to the house. Our newest cat is very talkative and fun.

Elvis (Captain Elvis)
My second white rat; rescued from a laboratory at Amy's college.

Grace Kelly (Moudy)
My first white rat. She would play with both Buttons and Ike. Sent packing for crimes against household furnishings.

Ike
Cocker spaniel, littermate of Mike. Ike was our first puppy after Malley. Sent packing for being allergic to Mom. (OK, perhaps it was the other way around.)

Katie (Kate-ma, Katherine, G-I-R-L)
Littermate of puppy friend, Dexter. Just adored Kirby. The only dog we have ever bred.

Kirby (Kirb-eee Pupp-eee, B-O-Y, B, Kirb Service)
First golden puppy for the Bors and me. He was truly special, loved Katie and the horses, and helped train Brownie and Standard. Laurie's dog of a lifetime.

Malley
My first dog. A cocker spaniel sent packing for who knows why.

Mike
Littermate to Ike. Belonged to our cousins who lived a half mile away from where I grew up.

Mitten (Mitta, Mee Dee, Mitta-mit-mit, MITT-en!)
The star of the show, to no one but me.

Mokie (Moke-Moke)
The shy, feral cat who sought refuge in the barn one tough winter. She grew to appreciate gentle strokes from Laurie, but remained shy around all other humans.

Muffy (May Jav)
The kids' puppy when they were growing up. She was such a little show dog and just so full of herself. Half Sheltie, all runt.

Naoz (Nubby)
Lowest maintenance cat we've ever had. Tiny, black and our current best all-around cat.

Nikka (Annika, Nick-L, Neek-o, Nikkapup)
Our current female golden. This nut is a perfect complement to our more regal Bailey. Named after Annika Sorenstam, the golfer.

Otis (Ot-ee)
Rob's college dorm stray cat. Oti found a great home with Shari and her family.

Papa (Mozart's Papageno)
Survived all of the early goldens, going back to the Kirby, Katie and Dexter days. Recently succumbed to old age; Papa and Sophie belonged to SLH and Patricia (not Morris), and stayed with us a few times.

Pogo and **Jet**
Two shelties we have cared for. Puppies of KMA, JWA and their boys. I think Jet sees me as a bone to perhaps chew on.

Pokay (Puck, Little Po, Punkin, Mah-jo-reen)
Age 23+, Laurie's cat of a lifetime.

Sasha
Amy and Nader's funny yellow lab, Sasha stayed with us for three weeks in 2007 and for over four weeks in 2008.

Scout (Scouty, Little Miss Scouty Pants, Scouty Pants, Miss Pants, Pants)
The most Mitten-like of all our current cats, and the smartest. Just a dickens.

Sophie
Another puppy name taken from opera, this SLH and Patricia golden was companion to Papa. She passed away too young.

Standard
Katie's other puppy; this one had a standard tan tummy.

Syd and **Jack**
Current goldens of MC, both dogs are from our breeder, Nancy. Jack and Nikka are littermates. They sometimes stay with us when MC travels.

Tanner
Service dog to our good friend Alicia, Tanner has also stayed with us. Loves Nikka.

Tubby (Tails)
Pokay's littermate. An orange tabby who bugged another orange tabby, the Mitten.

Twinkie Marie
Another ancient cat, lived 22 years. Belonged to NJO's family.

Walter (Batman)
The 100 lb. Bernese-cross belonging to Jen, Dave, Ella and Benny.

Two-legged characters

Alicia and **Tim**
Family to Tanner.

Amy (Amertile, Aima, Ima, Tile, Tiler, Im-the-tile, Armor)
Amy Jean Voedisch, daughter, doctor, age 33. Loves cats but hubby Nader has allergies. They now have a lab, Sasha, that Nader's eyes and nose can live with.

Barb
Barbara Jean Voedisch, the kids' mom (1946–2007).

Bors
See Laurie.

Bud
Co-worker at West. Marx Brothers or The 2000-Year-Old Man
. . . either fits.

Calfman (Sow 4)
Army pal from 1967. Master of Holsteins, husband to Carol.
No pets.

da da da dunt! (The Adams Family!)
Caretakers of Pogo and Jet.

Dad (Pop)
Frederic William Voedisch, 1903–1980.

Dan
Husband to sister Maggie (Meg); a couple of cat nuts.

DC
Bridge partner for many years; with wife Kay, owned another cat
named "Mitten."

DJ (Sow 1)
We started kindergarten together in 1949. Passed away from can-
cer in 2004. Jan was his rudder. When we were kids, Dave had
Duffy the puppy, while I had zilch.

Ella and **Benny** (ages 9 and 7)
With parents Jen and Dave, they are family to Walter Batman.
Ella and friend Nora operate Puppy Paradise, a pet care service
we have used.

JWA and **KMA**
Along with their boys, Stephen and Nicholas, the Adams family
has a couple of rambunctious shelties, Pogo and Jet.

Jon
Brother Jon Frederic Voedisch, 1939–1969.

Laurie (Bors, Lors, Lors-a-bors, Junior, Connie)
Partner in crime, spousal unit, and co-caretaker of the farm and
all the animals. She's tops!

Linda and the boys
Bors' sister, husband Rick, and sons Nick and John . . .
"da nephews." They have a dog, Murphy.

Maggie (Meg)
Sister, Margaret Alice Voedisch. With hubby Dan, two cat nuts.

MC
Good friend and total lover of goldens. She has had three goldens:
Dexter (littermate to Katie), Syd and Jack (littermate to Nikka).

Molly
Companion to Rob and also a writer; her father has severe cat
allergies so they could not keep Scouty.

Mom
Alice J. (Johnson) Voedisch, 1907–1981

Nader
"Mr. Amertile," young lawyer; has pet allergies but is a real trooper about it.

Nancy
Exceptional breeder of golden retrievers; provided us with Bailey and Nikka.

NJO (Queen Sow, Queenie)
Fine friend and cat nut; family cat was Twinkie Marie.

Ray (Shuey, Shuey, Shuey!)
Good friend; lives with his wonderful extended family in Utah; had a cat for 20 years, *the Judge.*

Rob (R-dub, Rels, Punk, RW)
Robert William Voedisch, son, teacher and writer, age 36. He and Molly want a rescue dog someday.

Ryebread and **Blepps**
Two *WESTLAW* sales reps who were introduced to the Mitten in a most crazy way.

Scrawn (Sow 2)
Met in grade school in '52; man of ideas, which sometimes actually work. When we were kids, he had Emil the cat. Marianne rides herd on the Scrawn.

Shari
Friend from West; loves animals; her family adopted Rob's Oti.

SLH and **Patricia**
Family to Papa and Sophie.

Z (Sow 3)
I met the Z in '56. Owner of many cockapoos. Bev tries to keep the Z in line. "That's all there is; there ain't no more."

CITIZEN Mitten

The recovery cat

The point is debatable, of course,
but I believe dog and cat lovers are generally made,
not born.

While planting shrubs in the front yard, my father suffered a massive heart attack and nearly died. It was the summer of '52 and Dad was rushed away in an ambulance. Nobody talked much about risk factors in those days, but at only 5 feet 9, and weighing 230 pounds, plus being a lifelong smoker and having a high-stress job, he was probably a walking coronary waiting to happen. He was only 49 and I can't imagine where I would be today if we had lost him then, when I was only seven and something. But through whatever medical means were available at the time, and by the grace of God, he survived. Mom always said we were so very fortunate he made it.

After what seemed like a month in the hospital, he had apparently reached the limits of recovery available from medical science, and home he came. He arrived in an ambulance and the crew lugged him upstairs and put him straight to bed, for what turned out to be many weeks of *bed rest*. In those days, the heart attack recovery process included bed rest and absolutely *no exercise*. The thought of actually getting up and using exercise to make the heart stronger was apparently unheard of back then. Even nuttier by today's standards, Dad was allowed to continue smoking so long as he switched to cigarettes with *filters*. How very odd; the medical community must have believed the cigarette ads on TV that claimed filters removed all the bad stuff. Good grief. The only thing they recommended that would make any sense today was a change to a low calorie diet so he would lose weight. This he did.

I'm just amazed Dad lived another 28 years. After three more, less severe heart attacks in his remaining years, Dad eventually succumbed to lung cancer in 1980. While Dad was in the nursing home waiting to die, his oncologist said, "Absolutely no smoking." After essentially a lifetime of smoking, Dad was not about to quit, cancer or not. He had his last cigarette the day before he passed away. Later on, you'll find out how he pulled off this bit of foolery.

So there was Dad, home again in 1952, but stuck in bed with nothing to do but read, listen to the radio, and work crossword puzzles. We ran meals up to him in bed because he wasn't to do anything but rest, and therefore, climbing stairs was out. We were the first on our block to have a television, but it was downstairs in the dining room, and Dad had to stay upstairs. Rats.

Why not move the TV upstairs? Two reasons. First, Mom hated the "tube" and would never stand for it being in the bedroom. Second, the thing had only about a 12″ screen but was in a cabinet the size of a small refrigerator, and it weighed a bunch. One idea was to move it upstairs each morning and back down each afternoon. Brother Jon and I rebelled. A second TV? Outrageous.

Here's a little sidebar on our early life with television. Vacuum tube technology didn't lend itself to compactness, but it did allow Dad to be his usual handyman self, both before his illness and after his recovery. If the picture was getting lousy, by the end of the week Dad would pull the back cover off the TV, either Saturday night or early Sunday morning before church, turn it on, and start removing any tubes that looked black or had a dim filament. Then, after church, it was down to the corner drug store to test the tubes on the green TV tube tester in the corner. You could plug a tube into its proper testing socket, and it would tell you if it was good or bad. If bad, there were replacement tubes right there in a rack near your head.

Another amazing piece of '50s technology was the foot X-ray machine at the local shoe store. It was there so you could check the fit of the new shoes before you took them home, but I recall it being used more to entertain one kid while the parent was buying shoes for the other. So as Mom was getting Jon fitted for oxfords or Maggie was trying on little saddle shoes, there I was, looking at my foot bones while wiggling my toes. I expect to die from bone cancer of the feet.

Of course if I don't die from this, I could possibly become careless and succumb to one of the "deadly seven." These are things I believe will send you to an early grave: *pasta, earth shoes, sushi, exercise, tofu, rice and tea.* Medical science will eventually prove each of these to be a killer, and you heard it here first. Speaking of food, why isn't one *cous* enough?

Where was I? Oh, right, Dad. His recovery was a real chore for him. How many murder mysteries can one guy read and how much CBS radio can you listen to? Options were limited: Arthur Godfrey, Art Linkletter, and soap operas. Even the local on-air personalities on WCCO, the Twin Cities CBS radio affiliate, with the unheard-of 60% local market share, weren't really that interesting after awhile. He listened to classical music on FM radio as well, and read the newspaper, in those days both the morning and evening editions, but nothing really helped as the days wore on.

What a snooze.

As Dad tired of books, radio shows and crossword puzzles, he came up with his own anti-boredom solution: *he wanted a kitten.* Mom gave in, perhaps somewhat reluctantly, and we got a "Holstein," a cute little black and white we called "Buttons." Actually, "Buttons Needles Voedisch" was his full name. We were big on middle names and "Needles" was sister Maggie's contribution. The kitten came from our very good friends, Bob and Miriam Russell of Deephaven, who lived in a classic old log home on Lake Minnetonka.

Buttons was Dad's cat and was such a good pal during this totally boring period in his life. They would play under the covers, and would sleep together in all sorts of positions and arrangements. Buttons would playfully bite Dad's feet, which would cause sort of a howling laughter from Dad. I remember Buttons biting Dad's pencil when he worked crossword puzzles which, rather than annoying Dad, would just make him chuckle. I just don't recall Dad ever getting mad at the little guy, except once when Buttons tipped over the Christmas tree a few years later. They were truly bonded; the best of friends. The rest of us loved the little guy not only for himself, but for how much he meant to Dad.

It was because of our little Buttons that *I became a cat person.* I wasn't the only one who caught the cat bug. Sister Maggie and her husband Dan in Oregon are just as cat crazy as we are, and have always had multiple cats. They have great cat stories.

Growing up in the '40s and '50s in the southwest area of Minneapolis was a kid's great fortune, which I realize now, but at the time, who knew? Minnesota is the "Land of 10,000 Lakes" (quite a few more than that, actually) and Minneapolis is the "City of Lakes." Up until the pro basketball team moved to Los Angeles in 1960, they were known as the "Minneapolis Lakers," winners of many NBA championships before blowing town. But you knew this, right? (I suspect if you're too young to know how to use a "church key" on a can of beer, you don't know about the Lakers' history either.)

Living two blocks from Lake Calhoun and three blocks from Lake Harriet, three blocks from a great little community shopping corner (no malls in those days, folks), three blocks from Lakewood Cemetery with its pond holding huge sunfish and bass (which we would fish for, illegally of course), a deep woods kind of park in the same direction, a scattering of vacant lots that would host our forts and battlefields, a short two-block walk to Lake Harriet grade school, and two blocks from the streetcar line for the really big trips, it really was a great neighborhood. This is known today by its trendy name of the "Linden Hills" area of Minneapolis, but to us it was just the neighborhood. We had everything a kid could want or need. If you've seen the holiday film classic, *A Christmas Story*, that's what our neighborhood kinda felt like, but with lakes and a sort of up-north feel with all the parks.

Dad said our house was built in 1905, a hardwood-floors-and-built-ins classic of sorts. It was roughly 30′ by 30′, with two full living floors: living room, dining room and kitchen down; three bedrooms and bath up; front and back porches, a two-thirds size finished attic, and full basement. Now why, as an almost empty-nester in 1968, Mom found it necessary to give away both my comic book collection and our Lionel electric train set because she needed "more room" in that big old house, I still ain't gettin'.

To show how far our society has advanced, or *declined*, in those days my mother thought nothing of letting me and another 8-year-old pal head downtown on the streetcar on a Saturday morning. First, we spent about two hours at one of our elegant and grand old movie theaters to see, probably in this order: cartoons, news-reels (major news stories in filmstrip form), a continuing serial that left you hanging with each 15 minute episode (and got you back into the theater a month later), and the main feature. Then over to shoot pool and play ping pong at the downtown YMCA, and have a candy bar and a pop. We returned home hours later, safe and sound. The amazing thing wasn't that we could do all this for less than a buck, it's that our mothers would let us do it at all. What mother would let her 8-year-old do this today in Minneapolis, or in any other major American city? She'd be arrested for child endangerment.

But life wasn't perfect. In our house, from 1949 to 1952, we had no pets. We had a dog when I was very little, a cocker spaniel named Malley. I can remember dressing her up in a T-shirt on a cold winter's day after the first big snowstorm. Then brother Jon and I stayed outside with her for what seemed like forever, making the huge pile of snow that would eventually be hollowed out to become the annual snow fort, an "igloo" that would last for months.

But Malley did dumb things in the summer, like sleep in the middle of Thomas Avenue, right in front of our house. Once, she was hit by a car, and maybe had a paw run over another time.

Mom and Dad decided she would be better off in the country. One of the men at Dad's office said he would take her to live on his farm, which happened in 1949. Talk about heartbreak for a four year old. I'm sure I cried for hours. I loved that dog, as did my older brother Jon, who always came up with the winter T-shirt uniform. At age two, little sister Maggie might have been too young to understand what was going on. As for me, I just don't ever remember getting a decent reason at the time for Malley having to go, and to this day, part of me still sort of questions the whole thing. They never said so at the time, but Mom's allergies might have been a factor.

Mom also had this thing for her nice carpeting and furniture and I remember her telling Dad that pets would ruin the house. I wasn't buying that one. But years later, she talked about how dogs and cats were bad for her "asthma." We kids eventually found out that the asthma thing was real, and Mom would sometimes really suffer. This might have been Malley's undoing.

In any event, after Malley we had no pets at all, while my neighborhood pals all seemed to have a dog or a cat, and some had *one of each.* I felt cheated and it bugged me. And I really missed Malley.

It wasn't until Dad's at-home recovery and the arrival of Buttons that I started feeling more like a normal kid.

Oak trees and acorns

They say the acorn never falls very far from the oak tree.
Sister Meg and I are about as goofy as Dad, and the kids,
Rob and Amy, are following along nicely.

Dad was a very smart guy, but he was also a real nut. I heard from many at his funeral that he was so intelligent but never took himself too seriously. He could be a goof at work and in social settings, not just around the house. More than one guy said Dad would disguise his brilliance with his comical side.

When we were little he would have us pull his finger so he could fart, showed us how to swallow air and do the schoolyard burp, and other prankish nonsense. His jokes and one-liners were classics. I can remember one of his lines from Mah Jong, a game Mom and Dad learned at college and taught us at an early age. When Dad was ready to Mah Jong (ready to go out), he would sometimes announce it like this: "O ye among you who have tears to shed, prepare to shed them now." I have since dressed it up for other settings by substituting "have cheese to cut" or "have ham to press" for "have tears to shed."

Of course it was my job to transfer all of this nonsense to the kids, which I have proudly done, along with a bunch of my own stuff. I could die with a smile tomorrow knowing I've corrupted them about as well as I could. Clear evidence came six years ago when daughter Amy was in her first year of Ob/Gyn residency and was assisting a surgeon. In the full-up operating room with Amy assisting, the surgeon, describing the procedure, made the comment: ". . . and if we can't do this the normal way, we'll have to go in through the rectum." To this, Doctor Amy replied from under her mask: "Rectum? Damn near killed 'em." Dead silence fell over the OR as Amy tried to retrieve her words that were now hanging heavy in the air.

With Amy perhaps thinking about her next career, eventually the head surgeon chuckled, others followed suit, and Amy's career as a doctor rose again from the ashes.

When I heard this I totally howled, and then I was filled with a great sense of pride, and thoughts about her grandfather. Dad would have gone wild.

Then there was this episode with 10-year-old Rob, who was playing at his best friend's house many years ago. John's family was strongly Catholic, something that was lost on Rob when he uttered during play, "Now that's enough to piss off the Pope." John's mother overheard this beauty and confronted Rob. "What did you say, young man?" at which point Rob, unsure of his exact crime, tried to cover his tracks with a sort of pleading question: "Uh, that's enough to *chafe* the Pope?" Ooops.

Yes, Dad, I have corrupted them well.

Passing on this legacy of craziness was not limited to just the kids. Every summer, Laurie's sister, Linda, would send her two boys from Washington State for a week at "the farm," and every year she would have to deprogram them upon their return. "Hey, Mom, who cut the cheese?" or "When you go to the movies, be sure to pick your seat," or peeing on the lawn or off the deck . . . all were probably relatively easy things to unlearn.

Other stuff was not so easy to undo. One summer I was sitting down with the nephews and asked if they had ever delivered a "moon shot." "What's that, Unca Biell?" I went on to describe the turning around and the dropping of drawers. They could hardly contain themselves. It was the following summer when I took it to the next logical step.

"You boys remember the 'moon shot,' right?"

"Sure, Unca Biell."

"Well, a special modification is 'pressed ham.'"

"What's pressed ham?"

"Men, that's the best there is . . . a 'moon shot' through glass."

They laughed and then asked "How does that work?" Ah, like fresh clay in my hands.

"You've got a patio door from your deck into the kitchen, right? You're outside; your Mom is inside. I'll let you guys work out the details." They went wild.

"But the best of all uses of pressed ham is *mobile pressed ham,* from a moving vehicle."

"Huh?"

I gave the highlights as best I could. One drives while the other moons; passenger side window up of course; a four-lane road or freeway so you can pull up alongside a car that is in the right lane and moon the driver with butt cheeks pressed against the passenger side window. It's best if it's someone you know. I thought this included enough of the basics to make the boys semi-dangerous upon their return home to Washington.

But even though they were giggling they still looked a little lost, and I thought they could use some visual help, an actual demonstration. So I pulled out the *American Graffiti* DVD. Using "scene select" they were soon watching the "Toad" getting his due from a passing car. The boys were on the floor. *Star Wars . . .* schmar wars! George Lucas nailed "mobile pressed ham" in *American Graffiti*, which I consider his greatest cinematic achievement.

To you dads and uncles out there, this is all good stuff, and way too important not to share with the youngsters, boys or girls.

By now, you're beginning to get the picture of Dad and me, he being the tree and me the acorn that didn't roll too far. The really fun part for me is that my acorns didn't fall too far away either, although they would protest otherwise.

Anyway, it should follow suit that, long before Mitten and I were being crazy together, Dad and Buttons were doing the same, as this story will show.

We were fooling with our morning Cheerios and toast when, from what seemed like the interior walls of the house, came a blood-curdling howl from our cat. Dad soon appeared from upstairs, ran down through the kitchen, and on down to the basement, laughing but in somewhat of a panic. He emerged from below a minute or two later carrying Buttons, whose ears were flattened, looking totally pissed. What the heck happened?

There was a corner clothes-chute to the basement from the second floor bathroom, a two-story drop. The chute emptied into a basket that sat on a table next to the washer and dryer. Dad liked entertainment when he was sittin' on the "growler," and not just reading material. He had a deck of cards in the bathroom for "floor solitaire." (I did a count once and found over 50 decks of cards in the house. We were raised on cards and Mah Jong.) That day, Dad was on the throne with Buttons in the growler-room with him, which was usually entertainment enough, I suspect. But this particular day Dad's growler entertainment took a crazy twist that cut short Buttons' enjoyment of the moment.

Once Dad caught his breath, he told the story. It seems Buttons was getting tired of playing "toilet paper hockey" on the bathroom floor, so Dad took the game up a notch. He tossed the wadded up toilet paper down the open clothes-chute . . . and Buttons followed! Dad really felt bad about this since he never dreamed Buttons would dive after it. He said he immediately regretted the whole thing.

We could only imagine the terror in the little guy, howling, claws out, scraping the sides of the metal chute all the way down, perhaps sparks flying . . . kerplunk, into the basket. I can look back and chuckle but at the time we were *not* pleased. Poor little Buttons. Dad tried to soften the story by saying there were clothes in the basket to cushion the little fellow's landing. Forget it.

This next story had us roaring. We were all inside doing whatever, except Dad. He came in the front door, his face bleeding, holding his broken glasses in one hand and Buttons in the other, all the while laughing like a goof. All right, what happened this time?

This episode was the old cat-up-a-tree dilemma. A stray dog had chased Buttons up the big elm in our front yard, and he wouldn't come down. I don't want to sound like Andy Rooney, but why is it when a cat goes up a tree, we think we need to help it come down? Why do we think cats can't figure it out for themselves?

So there's Buttons, maybe 15 feet or more up in the crotch of a pretty big elm tree, looking a little perplexed, I'm sure. Dad, of course, is going to help him down, but why bother with a ladder when all you have to do is gain the cat's trust to jump down and land on your back. Easy! Again, as described by Dad, there he was at the base of the tree, kinda bending over halfway, offering Buttons a flat landing spot on his back. He would bend over and, with his hand patting the top of his back, look back up at the cat and say encouraging words like "Buttons, jump . . . come on, Buttons . . . jump." He described how each time he coaxed Buttons, he would look back up at the cat. When he wasn't imploring the cat to jump, he would just stand still, bent over, waiting for Buttons to land on his back.

Dad must have miscalculated the whole glide and approach. The next time he looked up to continue the coaxing, there was Buttons coming right for his face, dropping like a rock, with paws and claws fully extended. Just like the episode with the clothes chute, once Dad stopped laughing he told the story, even as his face was shredded and still bleeding like a "stuck pig" (Mom's words).

Unlike the clothes-chute stunt, this time we really laughed. Of course it was Mom who had to doctor Dad's face, so the humor of the moment didn't really strike her. Moms are like that. They don't always see the full value of a situation since they're the ones who usually get stuck with the clean-up, in this case the doctoring of Dad's face. Dad taped up his glasses until he got a new pair.

Or this one. Dad loved his Christmas trees. Each year, it had to be the best one on the lot that we could afford, and once he had it up and at least somewhat plumb, he would march us to the tree for the family decorating event. We had a slug of decorations, including an angel that must have come over on the Mayflower (along with Louie Anderson's family Christmas tree stand), and really neat lights. He was partial to all blue lights, which is still my favorite, and Laurie's as well.

One year, just before Christmas, the tree was up and decorated in all its glory. Buttons was several years old and I wonder to this day why it took him so many Christmases to climb the tree. Up the trunk went Buttons, the tree became unbalanced and over it went. Pop was livid and tossed the whiskered gremlin out into the snow. But he just couldn't stay mad at his little pal, and I'm sure he went out and brought him back in just a few minutes later.

It was because of Malley and Buttons that I became first a dog person and then a cat person. For you non-cat types, you have no idea what you're missing. Once you bond with a cat, that's when the fun really begins.

Nearly thirty years after Dad got his cat of a lifetime, I got mine, a skinny orange tabby with an attitude, "Mitten." This book is our story, with some other related stuff thrown in for good measure.

How Mitten found me, or Runnin' the "drape relays"

If you're a cat, don't misbehave.
You might get moved, and your new home may or may not
be as good as the one you got kicked out of.

For whatever reason, for as long as I can remember, I have attracted stray cats. I think they can just sense a cat-friendly soul when they stumble on one. When we were growing up, stray cats would wander over to our house, but of course they couldn't stay. Mom wouldn't allow it. But later on in my life it became pretty routine for cats to show up, looking for a better deal than what they currently had. "Mitten the Kitten" was the first of many stray cats that found Laurie and me. He arrived in the fall of 1981.

These days, our vet, Dr. Steve, says that every time a cat finds us, it's like it has won some feline lottery. Of course, we always try to find the owner, but if that fails, we take the cat in for a full vet exam, neutering if it needs it, and shots. Then it's back to our farm for nothing but topnotch care until we can find a new home for it. And if we can't find a suitable new home, it stays.

The kids grew up on a farm about 20 miles northeast of St. Paul. This farm had built-in cats because the previous owner left a pregnant female behind. The litter was born in an old outhouse shortly after we moved in. What a circus as they grew and had the run of the farm. We soon found out that farm kittens do not have a very long life expectancy, and these little ones began to fade away. We suspected that some were carried off by dogs, or by the tough toms that patrolled the countryside. We did find homes for a few. We later learned that cats at many levels, from domestic cats to lions, sometimes have the breeding males kill off the local offspring to force the mothers back into heat. Eventually, the mother cat left.

A cat from that original litter, "Tony," was the kids' cat for most of their childhood. Mitten and Tony would have one encounter in the mid '80s that would send "Mittie" up a tree. Being sure Mitten needed my help getting down, but remembering Dad's hamburger face, I used a ladder.

Back to how Mitten found me. In 1980 I hired Laurie, a recent Augsburg College grad, to work in my group at West Publishing, which, at the time, was the world's premier legal publisher. Earlier, I helped lead a "skunk works" group at West as we moved the company out of the age of lead type into the new world of computerized typesetting, databases and *WESTLAW*, eventually the best, if not the first, online legal research service, which was launched in 1975. I had moved from the MIS department to the

WESTLAW division to lead most of the technical aspects of the system, plus Customer Service, where Laurie started her career.

I can still remember the interview. Her eyes were quite bright and her cheeks were very red. She later divulged that she had consumed a few beers the night before, and that she gets flushed when nervous, thus the red skin. She was also mighty cute.

There's an old saw in the printing business . . . "no dippin' into company ink," which basically means employees should not date each other. However, West was known for having two generations from the same family on the payroll, as well as many married couples. What the hell, I thought, once either of us got transferred to another department so that we no longer had a direct reporting relationship, all bets would be off and she'd be eligible.

Laurie was immediately seen as an up-and-comer and was plucked from *WESTLAW* Customer Service to help manage our massive computer operations section. In late 1981 I asked her out. Brrr, what a cold shoulder. But she warmed eventually and we began a somewhat secret thing. Our first date was to see the movie *Wolfen* at a theater in northeast Minneapolis, far away from "West Pub" and St. Paul, and from anyone who might recognize us. I had enjoyed the book of the same name and talked her into going. It was pretty good, actually. Of course, it's always a smart move to take someone to a horror film on the first date. She grabbed my arm during the scary parts.

I can still remember my boss, who found out four years later, in 1985, that Laurie and I were "an item." After a *lateral arabesque* within the company by me (my term for a company move that finds you elsewhere, but at the same level, without too much damage to your feathers), we were both in MIS at the same time, although not in the same group, and there was no reporting relationship between us. When our VP found out, he called me into his office and said something to the effect that we needed to keep the relationship outside the company, and be secretive. My comeback was swift and frank: "Boss, we've been dating since late 1981 and we'll be married next year . . . and *you* just found out about us. We must be doing something right!" That pretty much settled the matter.

About a year and a half after starting at West, Laurie was in an apartment with her roommate Janet, who, we found out later, was *not* a cat person. While doing laundry one day, Laurie found a young orange tabby, meowing up a storm, wandering in and out of the laundry room, rubbing Laurie's legs as cats will do as they either try to claim you or get you to do something, like give them a snack. This cat belonged to someone in the building, Laurie thought, so she made up signs and posted them around the apartment complex. She then made that fateful decision that would change all of our lives. She took him in, only "temporarily," of course, until the owner came forward.

I look back now at Mitten's craziness, and I can understand why his owner never claimed him. Mitten needed somebody new, someone who could understand him, who could tolerate him and who would love him dearly. *He needed* **me.**

So there they were, Laurie, Janet and Mitten. He didn't have his name yet, and they just called him "Kitty." The three of them tried to co-exist in a rather small two-bedroom apartment. It didn't take long for Mitten to show his stuff . . . he got into everything and had way too much energy. The final straw for Janet was when he went straight up the drapes, across the valance and down the other side, all in about four seconds!

That was it. Janet made it clear; it was either her or the cat. Laurie, not wanting to lose her roommate, asked if I would take the young man. I had been without a pet since Tony, so I said, "Sure, I'll take him." Although this was a decision I will never regret, it did prove to be quite a challenge for those around me — Laurie, Robbie and Amy — as we dealt with this little gremlin for many years to come.

So Mitten ("Kitty") moved in with me at the Laurel Apartments in the heart of St. Paul, across the street from the Commodore Hotel, long ago frequented by F. Scott and Zelda. I think this dramatic, historic location and my musty old apartment building just added to Mitten's mystique and his legend.

Mitten's shenanigans with Laurie and Janet actually worked in his favor, and he found a great setup with me.

Mitten and I were now together, for all time.

"Wherefore art thou Mitten?"

As a tribute to all of my high school English teachers,
Shakespeare enters the story.

Did you ever read *Romeo and Juliet?* I can remember 9th grade English class, when we tackled this dog. I have to say I was not a huge fan of the Bard, and like most squirts at age 14, found his works hard to read, a real chore. Sure, it was the language and style of his time, but for me it was work.

Take the balcony scene. "Romeo, Romeo! Wherefore art thou Romeo?" You read this and the first thing you think of is, hey, she wants to know . . . *where the hell is he?* No dice. As explained by our teacher, she is asking . . . *why* are you Romeo? The question is a lament without an answer, for if he were from any other family, their love would not be doomed . . . or whatever. That's what I remember, anyway.

24

Those of you accomplished in your understanding of Shakespeare will know if this is correct or not. For those of you who are not, what difference does it make? (My apologies to Victor Borge.)

Anyway, assuming I'm right, "Wherefore art thou Mitten?" would then mean, why are you Mitten? Or, perhaps, how did you come to be named Mitten?

This prompts a riddle from grade school:

Joe: Why do I call my dog Stretch?

Moe: I don't know. Why?

Joe: Cuz that's his name.

Once we decided we were keeping the little fellow, he needed a name. For some reason that I don't recall now, Laurie and I liked "Mitten." Not the more usual "Mittens," even though he did indeed have four white feet. We just thought "Mitten" somehow matched his unusual personality.

Oddly, the little runt was not the only cat named Mitten I have known. Pal DC, a regular bridge partner for over 30 years, along with some other smart guys, helped me become an ACBL Life Master in 1980. He and wife Kay also had a cat named Mitten. Not much similarity to my Mitten and, as I recall, was a reclusive female. I remember when they got a dog, their cat went into hiding and would not even come out for company . . . very un-Mitten like.

Little Amy put up quite a stink. She wanted any number of names: Bandit, Bunny, Bunny Bandit, Baby Bunny, Baby Bunny Bandit, Daddy Baby Bunny, Daddy Baby Bunny Bandit. Hmmm?

I tried to make a deal. "Amy, let's give him *five* names. Let's call him "Mitten Daddy Baby Bunny Bandit." Even at age five she was wise to my nonsense. Amy knew that the first name would be the "real" name, and she would have none of this baloney. Rats!

The next task was to have Amy choose a name to go up against "Mitten" in a household vote. She chose "Bunny Bandit" and I said no, that was two names and besides, it would be too hard to use. "Come, Bunny Bandit." Forget it. She settled on Bandit and actually, the orange and white markings on his face sort of looked like a mask. OK, fine. It was Mitten vs. Bandit.

This is where my memory needed some help from Rob, who remembers it vividly. We put it to a secret vote by secret ballot and I assumed it would go 3–1, but the truth is, somebody sided with Amy and we were deadlocked. According to Rob, we then came up with the idea that the only fair way was to *let Mitten choose his own name.* He liked to play with small things, so we took two plastic birthday candle holders, one pink and one blue, and we tossed them on the floor. Pink was for Mitten and blue was for Bandit . . . or was it the other way around? Whichever one he played with first, that was the name *he* picked.

We were squealing like betters at a racetrack. He eventually pounced on the pink one . . . or was it blue? . . . and he was then forever Mitten.

Little Amy was in tears, but when she calmed down, she sort of agreed it was fair. I suppose from her view at age five, life wasn't always fair, even when it was. Rob reminded me that later on, in a sort of protest, Amy renamed her stuffed bear "Daddy Baby

Bunny Bandit." At age 33, she still refers to her childhood bear as "Bandit."

A very good friend of mine, JWA, likes another name, "Mitchum." I never knew if he was a fan of the movie star or the deodorant, but he now barks out "Mitchum" in response to my somewhat musical "MITT-en." Our wives think we are basically bananas.

Later, I share more on the barking of Mitten's name.

"Quiet, Mitten.
It's Mrs. Johnson!"

The meow that almost sunk the ship.

The classic old Laurel Apartments in St. Paul was ruled with an iron fist by the elderly Mrs. Johnson. She and I got along fine until Mitten moved in, at which point our relationship went belly up. While dogs, small ones, anyway, were fine, she hated cats. But there was nothing in the lease that talked about pets at all . . . no prohibitions . . . so she set her own rules. Dogs were fine if they were small. Cats and large dogs were not allowed. These were Mrs. Johnson's rules.

Mitten would talk a lot, for no particular reason. Even when he was fat and happy, just had chow, taken a good dump and a whiz, and was well rested, he would still walk around the place and meow. I can remember the kids scolding him in a kind of strong whisper: "Quiet, Mitten. It's Mrs. Johnson!" Of course it didn't take long for Mrs. Johnson to hear the little fellow, and she came a-knockin'.

She would say either the cat had to go or I had to go, but our discussions about Mitten always ended the same way, by me saying something like, "Mrs. Johnson, there is nothing in the lease that says 'no cats.' There are no prohibitions against pets at all in the lease, and there are several small dogs in the building. As caretaker, you have tried to impose *your* animal preferences on the residents, allowing small dogs but nothing else, and you have no authority to do so. Have the owner of the building call me and I'd be pleased to discuss it further. Otherwise, there is nothing more to say on the matter."

I never heard from the building owner. Mrs. Johnson eventually gave up, and Mitten was in for the duration. He and I spent 4½ years at the Laurel.

The Laurel was such an interesting place in a rather odd neighborhood. We had an 80-year-old "paper boy" who would tear up and down the streets delivering papers. I swear he would walk 6 mph.

There were squirrels everywhere and, at times, they would sit on one of the window ledges of my first floor apartment and stare in. Mitten would go wild, making a cacking sound in his throat . . . "ack, ack, ack." He would just shake.

In 1981, I went to the boat show and bought a sailboat. Having no place to keep it, I bought a two-acre lake lot on Johnson Lake in northwestern Wisconsin, with a little 8 x 16 barn and a well, for a price that at the time, seemed pretty steep. A few months later, I bought the next bare lake lot to the south, also two acres. We lived in the little barn and this became our retreat, a place where we could all really crash, have fun, and just live. On weekends when we had the kids, it was a great improvement over the Laurel because there was just so much to keep us busy, especially the lake, of course. Laurie's two-bedroom deal with Janet just wasn't in the cards to be used by us, even when Janet was gone. But Johnson Lake was perfect, and we soon had a 1,200-square-foot cabin shell that, to this day, isn't totally finished.

We recently sold it to the fine young family with "Walter," a 100-pound Bernese, but we kept the second bare lot. The sale had to be OK'd by our kids, since it was really their second home all through their young years. Rob was fine and understood that it had become a chore to keep. Amy wasn't so sure but, eventually said fine, as long as our island cabin in northern Minnesota would get finished, with *full plumbing*. The Minnesota cabin is finally done, and for the first time since 1981, we can all go "to the lake" and go potty *inside,* and take a real shower, with *hot* water.

Once we had the Johnson Lake place, I could start collecting stuff again. There was a pile of lumber in the back of the Laurel, used but usable 2 x 12 x 16 footers. I called the owner and bought them all, not knowing exactly what I was going to use them for. We built a garage at the lake and stored them inside, along with two boats and two tractors. In 2005, maybe 23 years after I bought the used lumber, I gave it to Laurie's dad and brother for a project at the family farm. I just knew that lumber would come in handy.

I had accumulated some farm equipment that now could be moved to the lake, including two tractors and some machinery

— a two-bottom plow, disk, drag, and corn planter. Having over four acres at the lake provided a mini-farm of sorts right on the water, a really all-purpose experience. It was mostly sandy soil but our sweet corn crops were huge, plants nearly 10 feet tall with big, sweet ears. We would just let the neighbors pick their own, eat what we could, and bring some home to friends and neighbors, and for freezing.

The visitation arrangement was that I would have the kids every weekend, and up to two weeks in the summer. That was our time and it was pretty crazy, yet so special. In 1976, I had an apartment at the historic Commodore Hotel, a block from the Laurel. The Commodore was an efficiency apartment but it had a really big closet where I stuck a small bed for Robbie. Amy was in a crib next to my bed. What a time to be alive. We would go all sorts of places together: to Mom and Dad's, grocery shopping, out for a meal, a movie, the zoo, to Menard's (like Home Depot), a big toy store, down to the river or a park . . . it didn't matter. I was just always carrying little Amy and her bag of supplies . . . diapers, baby wipes, a formula bottle, a pacifier. I was tired, yet so fulfilled by Sunday night, when it was time to drive them back. That's when big tears would flow almost every time after I dropped them off. My lawyer made it pretty clear: custody by me was not going to happen and weekly visitation was about as good as I could expect. Barb was very supportive on this point, that the kids and I really needed our time together.

It was the stretch at the Laurel and at the cabin (1981–1986) that we remember as the "early Mitten years." Laurie was almost always with us and they were such great times. I would play a little game with the kids. Each Sunday night, as we were driving back, I would ask . . . "OK, kids, what was the highlight of the weekend?" to which they would *always* respond in unison . . . "Going home!" . . . just to give me a bad time.

Mitten would always go with us to the cabin on weekends. The problem was, he *hated* traveling.

Head butts and nursing stations

With cats, I think there's a nurture vs. nature conundrum afoot.

We want to believe that cats have all sorts of ways to show us true affection. Take the head butt. A cat can be standing on your chest, purring up a storm as you are lying in bed, and push its head right into your chin, cheek or forehead, rubbing mightily, while purring away. We see this as a sign of affection, the cat's way of hugging us or whatever. I think it generally is, but there could also be an instinctive, territorial aspect to it as well. Apparently the little characters have scent glands in their cheeks, so when they do the big rub with the side of their face, they could just be "marking" us as belonging to them. How stale.

I suppose being "marked" might not be too bad, but being "hugged" seems so much better.

They weave in and out of our legs in the kitchen, rubbing us while purring. Are these "hugs" or just prompts for us to serve up some cheese from the fridge? We like to think they are showing us tons of love when it might just be the leftover chicken that is causing this behavior.

Do you cat owners have "nursing stations?" Let me explain, and it has nothing to do with hospitals. If you're a cat person you know that these little goofballs can sometimes revert to their babyhood and "nurse," like when they knead on your shirt with their paws and claws, back and forth, and then suck or lick on the fabric, like baby kittens.

Nursing on your sweatshirt is one thing, but nursing on your body parts is quite another. The sandpaper tongue and tiny front teeth will drive you nuts. I call these favorite body parts cat "nursing stations." Mitten had several on me.

In my life of many cats, only three have "nursed" on me. Tubby, who along with Pokay, was rescued from Laurie's family farm in 1984. He would nurse right on my chest, generally in the middle of the night. I'm a wooly guy, body-hair wise, and my chest must have reminded him of "mom." Of course it wasn't just the sandpaper tongue, it was his paws and *claws* kneading back and forth into my skin. Eee-youch! I would wake up, of course, and the only way I could let him continue was to hold his paws with my thumbs so at least the claws were out of my chest.

Scouty (little Miss Scouty Pants) is one of our five current cats, four of whom live in the house; the other is a barn cat. Scouty is the most Mitten-like of any cat I've ever been around since the Mitten's passing in 2000. She nurses right on my beard and can go non-stop for minutes at a time. She doesn't do the paw-kneading, so it's tolerable. Still, her sandpaper tongue is murder on my face. More on Scouty later.

Mitten found the most unique nursing station of all, my ear lobes. Part of the nursing ritual is purring, and when the little nut was nursing on my earlobe, his nose was almost in my ear. His purring, right into my ear, was like an old prop plane idling on the tarmac. Laurie would say it was cruel of me to stop him, but sometimes the pain of his nursing, plus the noise in my ear, was more than even I could bear, and I had to fend him off . . . but back he'd come. My ears were red and sore after these bouts, but it was Mitten, and I had a ton of patience for this and many of his other crazy routines.

After all, he was my boy.

Cats have scent glands in their feet as well, so they can leave their mark on tree bark and such in the wild. So when they are kneading away on our guts, are they using us as a substitute "mom," or are they trying to tell the next visiting cat that we are already spoken for?

I say let's make ourselves feel good, dismiss the notion that all of this fun behavior is strictly instinctive, and go with the affection thing.

You know, kinda like our assumption that a cat in a tree absolutely needs our help.

The bad traveler

We always thought that leaving cats at home on the weekends
we went to Johnson Lake was a bad deal for the cat.
Oh sure, a cat can manage two days with a clean litter box,
water and a pile of food, but it just seemed unfair.
Besides, why wouldn't they want to come along?

Why, indeed!

In the early days of Johnson Lake I had a Mazda pickup truck, which had about as small a cab as you could find on any vehicle except a sports car. Even a VW bug had a back seat. So it was the four of us abreast across the front, or Amy sitting on Bors' (Laurie's) lap. We also had two animals to take along: Mitten and the kids' adorable, half-sheltie/half-something-with-short-legs, "Muffy." By the spring of '84 we had added two more kittens, Pokay and Tubby.

How do you transport two adults, two kids and four pets to the lake, about an hour and a half drive, in a Mazda pickup truck? The kids laid down the law: "Muffy rides in the cab of the truck." That left the three cats in the pickup bed in cat carriers. We put Tubby and Pokay in one larger carrier and Mitten in a smaller one. If we thought it might rain or if it was cold, we would wrap the cat carriers in a tarp or blanket

Mitten hated the whole concept of traveling. We would stop for gas or groceries and he could be heard howling something awful from inside the carrier. People walking by would look at us like we must be beating the cat to death. Blood-curdling howls. Embarrassing, actually.

By the time Mitten got to the cabin he was so chapped he wouldn't have anything to do with us for an hour or so . . . he would just sulk. But, eventually, he would snap out of it and start settling in. That was Friday night. Saturday was generally fine, although he would get into all sorts of trouble, like crawling into unfinished spaces or going up into the rafters, climbing over the top of the wall and running inside the soffit area. He showed us there were lots of places a cat can hide in an unfinished lake cabin.

Sunday was another story. He did the math early and realized that by Sunday it was soon going to be time to go home — and another awful ride. *So he'd run away!* More than once, he just tore off into the woods and we could not find him. By 5 p.m. we had to go. If Mitten was still AWOL, all we could do was put a dish of cat food and a water bowl on the picnic table on the deck, and go home. That happened more than once. I would have to go back up on the following Tuesday or Wednesday and find the little goof. Sure enough, I'd go back up a couple days later and he'd be right there, sitting on the deck, looking for all the world like everything was just fine. "You little sow."

This led to the "Sunday Mitten Rule." Past noon on Sunday the little shit was **not** allowed outside the cabin for *any* reason. With his quickness and cunning ways, this was often a real challenge.

Pokay gave us the biggest scare, however. One Sunday we could not find her, and since she had never done anything like this before — running away at the cabin — we were very worried. We put out food and water, and then we had to leave. Laurie made a sign, "Missing Calico Cat" with our home phone number, and nailed it up on a tree at the entrance of the dirt road that led to our end of the lake. Pokay was her little girl and Laurie was crying as we drove away.

I encouraged the Bors to go back up on Tuesday and start checking cabins, garages and sheds. Pokay was such a scaredy-cat that I thought she could have been frightened, and had run inside someplace. Laurie went back up but there was no Pokay waiting by the cabin. So she began walking around the neighboring cabins and garages, calling for her Pokay and then listening for her cry. Sure enough, Pokay called back to her from inside a neighbor's garage. She was up high, like in the soffit overhang area.

Bors ran to our cabin for some tools and a short ladder, then back to the neighbor's garage. She began talking to Pokay again, who joyfully talked back. There was a soffit light about where Pokay seemed to be, so Bors took out the screws and pulled the light down a bit, and out came a little white paw. Laurie said she started to cry tears of joy. But there was still work to do . . . Pokay could push her head out the light hole, but her body would not fit through. Bors had to pull down some of the soffit plywood before she could get the little purr-box all the way out.

Once Pokay was out, the Bors nailed everything back up, screwed the light back in and started back to the cabin with the ladder and tools. Pokay never left her side and talked to her non-stop, as if to share her adventure. This neighbor had a dog and we speculated it chased Pokay inside their garage sometime that Sunday. Laurie was sure Pokay was trying to tell her the whole story. A chipped tooth from the adventure is her badge of courage. Perhaps she tried to chew her way out.

As I sit here at my computer in the office writing this book, Pokay is curled up beside me on the desk, in one of those soft cat-nap round mini-beds, purring up a storm. At age 23 and 8 months, she is still going strong. More on Pokay later.

Tubby had a classic Johnson Lake experience. He had no particular fear of water and would go right down to the lake for a drink and then a walk on the dock. Mitten and Pokay hated the dock, thinking, I'm sure, they would fall in. Our last four dogs, not counting the mixed stubby-legged Muffy, have been golden retrievers, who loved the water. Tubby perhaps thought he should have been a golden.

One day he was on the dock and thought he should get into the canoe which was tethered to the dock. He put his paws on the gunwale of the canoe, but rather than jumping in, he really didn't do much of anything. His body weight on his front paws slowly pushed the canoe further away from the dock until . . . ker-plunk, he was in the drink. Laurie said he shot out of the water on his own and back onto the dock, all in one motion. His ears went flat and he was plenty chapped. A quick toweling off and he was good as new, but he never went on the dock again.

Cats at the lake cabin . . . a fun, yet sometimes interesting, combination.

Now it's time for some pictures.

Our family: Dad, Jon, the author, Maggie and Mom

Buttons, the recovery cat

Pokay and Mitten help inspect the catch

Mitten sniffs the finished goods

"IN or OUT, young man?"

Katie, Kirby and the dancing Mitten

The author, Amertile and Tubby

Standard and Brownie

A boat ride can make your ears "wing"

"Don't forget me!"

Kirby meets Maggie . . .

. . . and then Loki

A fine combination: calves and goldens

Kirby, Katie and friends at a Humane Society dog walk

Mr. Nice Guy...

...Mr. Grumpy Pants

We share some chicken

Rafter cat

Katie was certified for scuba diving

Bailey had a ski pass

Bors & Pokay, me & the Mitten, Amy & Tubby, Rob & Muffy

Katie with Bors and Pokay . . . me and the Mitten with Kirby

We bring home Bailey . . .

. . . and later, Nikka

Nikka's first Christmas

Pokay on the desk, helping me write

Scouty and Earl

little Naoz

Christmas card picture reject

ditto

Tubby dozes on Mitten

Remembering those who have gone before

Hizzonor tolerates a dog

Mittie digs for treats

Citizen Mitten avoids the badgering newcomer, Bailey.

Citizen Mitten

Author's self-portrait

Author's portrait of Mitten

60

Mitten goes to a sales meeting

Rule 72: Never take a cat to a sales meeting.

If I did a little research, I suppose I could come up with the history of the cats-having-nine-lives thing. Myth or whatever, Mitten burned up a few in some of the most bizarre and crazy ways. One such episode was Mitten at a *WESTLAW* Sales Meeting. Being involved with *WESTLAW* for most of my 26-year career at West Publishing Company (which became West/Thomson, then Thomson/Reuters something or other), attending sales meetings and giving presentations on our technology and database enhancements, and the latest on *WESTLAW* vs. *LEXIS* (our competitor), were part of my duties for a number of those years.

One such summer meeting was to be held at Cragun's Resort in northern Minnesota, a beautiful place on a great vacation lake in a north woods setting, with golf courses, fine food and excellent facilities. I needed to be there for three nights and three days, longer if I wished, and I needed someone to take care of the little guy. Laurie was gone that week and I was not about to farm him out to a cat kennel deal . . . how cruel. I tried to find someone to come in and feed him, change his litter box, and maybe play with the little fellow. Even though this would be pretty boring and lonely for Mitten, it seemed the best course. But I just couldn't find anyone I could trust on what was fast becoming short notice.

The eventual solution? . . . I'd take him along.

He slept much of the way on the drive up, but got a little owl-y toward the end of the three-hour trip. I stopped at a fish shop near Brainerd and got him some smoked whitefish. He thanked me by being fairly calm for the final 30 minutes on the road. I had a litter pan for him right in the car, and he used it just before we got there. Uff da. It was windows down that last five miles.

I was assigned to a three-bedroom bungalow with two of my favorite *WESTLAW* field dudes, Ryebread and Blepps . . . not their real names, but their real West nicknames. Of course they had no idea "his craziness" was coming along, so that was my first chore, informing the boys that we were a foursome. Would they mind? If either was allergic to cats or had a complaint, Mitten and I would just get a single room in the lodge. Their attitude? What the hell, no problem. Of course, they had never met the Mitten, and they were about to get a real introduction.

So, how much trouble can one cat get into? Plenty, and Mitten even surprised me on this particular trip.

To start with, he fell in love with the assortment of shaving kits in the common bathroom. He'd dig into these things with plenty of zeal and would drag stuff out and carry it around in his mouth. A cat carrying a razor around in his chops looks pretty goofy.

We had some snacks on hand. He found those that were not in the fridge and ate right through the bags. OK, all pretty tame stuff so far, I suppose.

He was at his best, however, when it came time to explore. Going room to room, he eventually ran out of new things to play with. He went back to what had become his favorite room, the "growler," and started to really sniff around. Our cabin had central forced-air heat, with ductwork running under the cabin crawl space into each room. One heat duct terminated in the bathroom with a somewhat cheesy vent grill covering the duct. Mitten the Kitten learned that if he dug his claws behind this grill and tugged, off it came.

I found it off the first morning, so I put it back on. I should have asked for some tools to secure it, like a couple of long screws, but instead, I just shook my finger at the little shit and scolded him. "Leave the heating grill alone, young man!" I barked, as I pointed to it. He looked at me like I was from Mars.

We were in meetings most of the first full day and I didn't get back to the room until about 5 p.m. Blepps was already there and he had a funny look on his face. When I asked what was up, he said that Mitten had taken a little trip . . . into the ductwork under the cabin! Good grief.

I went to the bathroom and, sure enough, the vent cover was pulled off again, and Mitten was gone. I got down on the floor on all fours and listened. I could hear him inside the ducts, moving around. I called for him and heard his faint meow. My fear was that he was lost in the maze of duct work and couldn't find his way back. He began to meow a ton. I would try to call him back to the bathroom, but no luck. He just kept answering me with faint meows. I was crushed.

Now what?

After awhile, Ryebread showed up and the three of us puzzled about it a bit, but nobody had any ideas. I had a little whitefish left in the fridge so I put some down into the bathroom duct, hoping the smell would attract him. Ryebread, Blepps and I went to dinner but when we came back, there was still no Mitten and the fish hadn't been touched. When Mitten heard us, he started the faint meows again. I was getting seriously bummed.

I then had to ask the boys for a *huge* favor . . . would they mind if I turned the thermostat way down, essentially disabling the furnace. It was July, but northern Minnesota can still get a little nippy at night. I just didn't want the furnace kicking in, scaring the crap out of the little fellow, then roasting him. Or worse, having him go the wrong way and tear headlong into the furnace fan. Who knew what might happen, or what he might do? Blepps and Ryebread were troopers and agreed. To this day I am in their debt.

After a bump of sour mash on the rocks, I checked the ducts one last time before I went to bed. Still no Mitten. I didn't sleep very well and did some sobbing into my pillow.

The next morning I got up, went out to the kitchen, and there was Mitten, looking like a fugitive from a dustmop convention. I cried as I cleaned off the sticky cobwebs and dust bunnies. He was a mess, but he was fine, and mighty happy to see me, purring like crazy. I thought of Pokay and the Bors and their Johnson Lake adventure. Of course the Bors cried when she found Pokay, just like I was crying now. It was soon "nursing station" time on my ear lobes, a true sign of his affection. I decided to take it, and just let him punish my ears with his sandpaper tongue and little front teeth. My Mitten had come back.

I'm sure the sales boys thought the two of us were nuts.

That was Mitten's first — and last — sales meeting.

The boxing cat

Your cat may have an athletic calling.
Encourage it.

Y ou've heard of a boxer dog. Mitten was a boxing cat. We think this is a rarity since he's the only cat we've ever known who "boxed." When Mitten boxed it was always a fair fight. He never used claws, just the pads of his paws. He was like a feline Mohammed Ali, with lightning quick punches.

He would "box" only when upset, and his startled opponent could be man or beast. The two victims I recall were the Bors and the neighbor's dog at Johnson Lake. The dog, a nice lab mix, was black with a white tuft on his chest. "Panda," a really good boy, wandered over one day for a visit. When he came over, Mitten got irritated. The dog was doing no harm at all and was being good pals with our pups. This made no difference to Mittie, who growled and glared at the visitor. When that didn't drive him home, the little butt charged Panda, who then started running toward home. Mittie hopped on his butt as he was running, delivering a barrage of blows, first one paw then the other, in a rapid-fire blur. You could hear the quick thumps of Mitten's paws on poor Panda's hindquarters. After a brief ride, Mittie jumped off and came back, with his ears flat and eyes looking a little crossed. "So there!"

What a poor host.

The best boxing attack occurred some time earlier when he was being held by Laurie in front of her duplex in St Paul. When we lived in town, before we built our first farm, we never let our cats outside, fearing dogs, traffic, or a cat just running away. So it was a real treat for Mittie when he escaped through an open door, scooted downstairs and outside. Mitten had a brief tour and Laurie went out to get him. As she was carrying him back to the front door, she stopped to talk to the downstairs tenant for just a minute or two.

Being held by the Bors as she shot the shit with a neighbor was not what the Mitten had in mind. He turned grumpy and before Bors knew what was going on, Mitten landed a rapid volley of punches on either side of her face. The neighbor woman went wild with laughter as Laurie got the hint and took him immediately upstairs. She called me at work and tried to tell the story, but she was giggling so much she had a hard time getting it out.

The kids were never subjected to the little guy's pugilistic skills, at least that we know of, or that they would admit to.

As you talk to cat owners, ask them if their munchkins have ever "boxed." It's hard to believe Mittie was the only cat to ever do this, but he was a total nut, so who knows?

A boxing cat is a riot to behold.

The best defense? . . . flat ears!

How can a brightly marked calico think she can simply crouch down in green grass and not be seen? Such is the behavior of our Scouty Pants, and before that, our orange and white Mitten.

We think Mitten wanted to be an outdoor cat, but it was usually a bad match. Even on warm days he generally would not stay out for any length of time. He wouldn't wander far and actually wanted us outside with him. More than once he'd howl at the screen door but when we opened it to let him out, he'd run 10 feet, look back and meow, as if to say, "Please come out and play."

When his time outside was done, he'd do the reverse. He'd howl and try to lead us back to the house so he could go in. Everything was on his schedule. But he was kind of a wimp outside, even in the nicest summer weather, and he rarely stayed out past dark. He was a nervous sort, to be sure, plus he had a thin coat of fur that wasn't much help on cool nights, and was just about useless in the winter. That, and perhaps his near-death experience with the killer trout, made him a winter-wimp. More on the killer trout later.

Tubby, on the other hand, would take off for two or three days at a time, sometimes in the dead of winter.

Mitten had two outdoor stunts that, to this day, we recount with a smile. Both had to do with that hilarious feline secret move, *ear flattening*. Whether for stealth or avoidance, or just to express complete annoyance like when he boxed, Mitten would flatten his ears. He would do it without fail during two situations outdoors.

The first was when Mittie was the target of dive-bombing swallows. Mitten liked to roll in the gravel driveway out in front of the horse barn. We'd call him "roll cat" since he would do it with such gusto. He'd roll back and forth so hard there was a little dust cloud over him. Of course, his orange tabby fur became gray with the stuff.

The barn swallows would spot Mitten on the gravel driveway and start swooping down toward his head, coming ever closer, even hitting him at times. Mitten would crouch down and then hold his position. As a diving swallow came close to his head, he would drop his head, maybe half an inch at most, and then *flatten his ears*. This could go on for ten minutes or more, with several birds involved. We would crack up.

His second use of ear-flattening would happen while we all went for a walk. Anyone can walk their dogs on their farm, and we would too, but we would also walk our *cats*. Many times in the early farm days of the late '80s and early '90s, all three cats would join us for a walk, but they were very different from the dogs. Dogs wanted to lead, would get well out front, wander back and forth, and often had to be called back from the wetlands and burr patches, with limited success. Our cats, on the other hand, would walk behind. We would walk for a minute or so, turn around and there they were, trotting behind. Tubby and Pokay would trot after us, with Pokay meowing to let us know she was coming. But Mitten turned this into a game of sorts. His job? Spy! When we turned around he would immediately lay flat *and flatten his ears so as not to be seen.*

All he needed was a tiny trench coat, dark glasses and some little buildings to duck behind. "Stealth Mitten, secret agent."

Now how stealthy can an orange tabby be in green grass? He was such a nut. Our beautiful calico, Scouty, now pulls the same stunt, "hiding" from our dogs in the mowed lawn until they get close, then springing up to attack their ears or rear end. Of course they see her every step of the way.

Ear flattening . . . a cat's secret weapon.

The killer trout

A small trout can gobble a dragonfly nymph,
but could it dispatch a house cat?

Mitten's nine lives were tested in some very odd ways, but none more improbable than the episode of the *killer trout*. This goes back to our Laurel Apartment days. One winter night, I went to the Sportsman's Show with two old friends, Scrawn and Z. This is one of those dead-of-winter-so-let's-think-summer shows that are held in the far north, and probably elsewhere as well.

I met the Scrawn when I was in third grade, in 1952. He was a year ahead of me in school and even though we only lived a block apart, I didn't really know him. We met when I sheepishly asked him to ask his older brother to stop beating me up. It worked, and we became fast friends.

I met the Z when we started seventh grade. Scrawn, then an 8th grader, linked up with Z at our new junior high school, and Z fell right in with the crew. That was 1956. I still bum around with these guys today, 56 years later for Scrawn, 52 years later for Z, and they were not even my oldest friends. That honor went to DJ, with whom I started kindergarten in the fall of 1949. After a 55-year friendship, I gave a eulogy at his funeral in October 2004, following his 20-month battle with cancer.

The four of us hung around together all those years, and I'm still hangin' with Scrawn, Z, and Calfman, the new kid who joined us in 1967. I am blessed for sure.

Z has introduced a new dude into the mix, Bo, a fellow employee at the Minnesota Department of Transportation. Bo, being basically bananas, fits right in.

Like Ryebread and Blepps, the sales meeting dudes, Scrawn, Z, DJ, Calfman and Bo are their real nicknames but their given names shall be kept a mystery.

We didn't always have to go hunting or fishing to have a good time. Besides the card games, cutting firewood and the nutty projects, we would go to the winter "shows." Nothing will ever match the Sportsman's Show of 1961 when you could pay $2.00 to wrestle "Victor the Rasslin' Bear." Z and I ponied up a buck each so the Scrawn could match hammerlocks and half nelsons with what was surely a 500-pound black bear. Scrawn wasn't going to do it unless we paid the entry. I will tell you this: based on just pure entertainment value, it was the best buck either of us has ever spent. I thought we were going to die from laughter.

Scrawn's plan was to grab Victor by a rear leg and tip him over. They did a few friendly pushes and the brute tossed Scrawn to the mat a time or two. Then Scrawn saw his opening and went for one of Victor's rear legs and started to lift it up. Victor became annoyed and simply laid down, flattening the Scrawn. Z and I were dying, barely able to hold each other up. Afterwards, Scrawn kept mumbling, "My foot slipped or I coulda beat that tub." We just laughed all the more.

Then there was the 1985 Sportman's Show where I purchased the "Ginsu" knives. Oh sure, you can laugh, but it's 2008 and I still have these things, and they have never needed sharpening, just like the guy said. One is in the butcher-block knife holder in the kitchen and the other two are in toolboxes. What more can you ask of a product?

Anyway, in 1984, Scrawn, Z and I were headed to the Sportman's Show in St Paul. Just inside the door, the first thing you saw coming in and the last thing you saw going out, was a fishing pond stocked with trout. On our way out there was quite a commotion around the canvas pool. It seems the aerator had quit and the trout were going belly-up. The two guys running the thing were selling barely live trout in baggies for 50 cents each. I talked the guy into three for a buck.

Of course, Scrawn and Z thought I was nuts. I didn't tell them that I was going to do a trout dinner for Laurie. This was before we were married and my theory was that an occasional nice meal at my place, cooked by me, might keep her interest from going the way of an un-aerated fish in a green canvas tank.

As I recall, the meal was trout, broccoli, French bread, and a half giraffe of wine. You may be more familiar with the full giraffe of wine, the decanter with the longer neck.

When I got back to the apartment, Mitten immediately smelled the fish and went wild. He meowed non-stop and followed me straight to the kitchen. He stretched up on my leg and dug his claws through my pants into my skin. "What the hell! Lay off, you little runt." He could not contain himself. I gutted and gilled the fish, added some water, sealed the baggie as best I could and tossed it in the freezer. Then I took the garbage with the fish guts down to the dumpster in back. Whew! When I got back, Mitten continued to walk around the fridge and wouldn't stop purring, so when he'd meow it was that great half-purr, half-meow thing that was always so funny. "P-u-r-r-r-e-o-w!"

He and I watched a little news and then went to bed. I always preferred Mitten up under my arm when we slept. If he curled at my feet it was fine until I moved in the middle of the night. More often than not, moving my feet bothered him, and he would bite my feet right through the covers. Keeping him in a loose head-lock up near my chest was best. But he was still very interested in the kitchen, and trotted in there again before I dozed off.

Mitten had a continuing keen interest in the kitchen and the fridge after the trout came home, especially when I had to open the freezer. He went nutty each time. The trout odor, even frozen trout, must have been like catnip to him. It was not too many nights after the trout arrived home that they got the better of my little whiskered friend.

I woke up around 3 a.m. to faint meows. It was Mitten, but it was like he was not in the apartment. *Where the heck is he?* I looked out in the hall . . . not there. Even though it was February, I opened a window (it was a ground floor apartment) to see if he had gotten outside and was perhaps on the window ledge right outside the apartment. These were not foolish checks on my part since he had escaped in the past, a few times out into the hall and once all the way outside. He was like a little Houdini.

Nothing. I wandered the apartment and could hear his faint cries. They were the loudest in the kitchen. I searched behind the stove with a flashlight and I even opened the oven. No Mitten. I was standing there in my boxer shorts and T-shirt, looking at the fridge. Could he have somehow gotten up inside the rear of the thing, trapped next to the condenser or something? I pulled the fridge away from the wall a bit, got down with the flashlight and looked up into the rear of the unit. Nothing.

So there I am, once again standing in front of the fridge, looking at the damn thing, and telling myself . . . no way is he in there. But I just had to check.

I opened the lower fridge door . . . no Mitten. Like a robot, I opened the top freezer door . . . and *out he came* . . . leaping onto my neck and hanging on for dear life. He was scared, cold and perhaps not far from death. I have no idea how long he had been in there . . . maybe an hour . . . maybe more. I really didn't know.

We went straight to bed and he curled up on my chest, under the covers, and never moved. He purred for the longest time and finally went to sleep. I stroked him for as long as I was awake. From that point forward our bond was . . . if I can paraphrase a line from John Candy in *Planes, Trains and Automobiles* . . . tighter than Tom Thumb's *butt.*

I checked out the freezer door the next day. The magnets holding it shut were pretty weak, and Mitten was a pretty smart cat. I could just imagine him seeing the freezer door open a few times, and figuring out how to open it himself. All he had to do was get on top of the fridge and push against the top edge of the freezer door with his paws, open it and crawl in. Of course, the door closed behind him and he was then in *huge trouble.*

I've generally been a light sleeper and Mitten was always a loud meow-er. That combination, and my silly "What would Mitten do?" thinking on that night, prevented my little guy from becoming a victim of the *killer trout.*

This is just as it happened but, alas, there are no living witnesses but me. May I be forced to eat my weight in tofu, couscous and polenta if this is not all true.

The Bors thought the trout dinner was fine. She gave some of hers to little Mitten, just to shut him up. That seemed fitting . . . Mittie eating one of his would-be assassins.

"IN or OUT, young man?"

Cats are smart, but sometimes they
just can't make up their mind what to do.

Mitten had the scrawniest coat of any cat I've ever been around. He was always well groomed and looked sleek, but too sleek, really. He was never more than 8 lbs. "soaping wet" (per little Amy), and he looked it. Other cats of similar weight looked fatter because they had some semblance of what Robbie would call that "Frankenstein" look, a wooly coat. Not the Mitten.

Thin is in? Fine, if you're a Paris runway model, but for a cat in Minnesota, a thin look is *not* the best, especially during our long, cold winters. We measure winters not so much in terms of snow on the ground but by ice on the lakes. "Ice on" might happen any time in November and "ice out" for a typical lake could happen any time in April, but more like early May this year, 2008. That's our five months or more of winter, when we have "hard water."

What can really freak out someone from the South, California, or any warm climate, is driving on a frozen lake in January. It usually goes something like this:

"Undo your seat belt and roll down your window."

"Why? It's freezing out."

"In case we go through, you don't want to be strapped in, and your escape route is the window . . . **not** *the door*. Never open the door, that just sinks the vehicle faster."

Pause . . . "Can we go back?"

Mitten, like most cats, wanted to be outside, and for seven months of the year, it worked fairly well for him to be out for relatively short periods. But, as I've mentioned, even cool summer nights were often too chilly for his miserably thin coat.

Outside for cats should be a good thing. Their "growler" (family talk for the bathroom as well as the stool itself) expands from a small litter box to the whole world. They can play detective, chase a mouse, eat a bug and generally revert to their ancient instincts. Tubby loved it because he would double his food intake. Not only was he a good "mouser" but he loved insects. Once, when we were at the cabin, he was crouched down low, and turned to look at me when I called his name. There he was, a dragonfly tail sticking out of one side of his mouth with the wings sticking out of the other. He looked a little wild, actually, maybe like a lion with an antelope leg.

Mitten, like any cat, had his own outside rituals and haunts, like tempting the swallows to dive bomb his head. But as October approached, his trips out would get shorter and shorter, based solely on the colder weather. He just couldn't take it.

Winter was a real challenge for him. He wanted to go out, but couldn't, at least not for more than a minute or two. Thus, you would often hear me, Bors or the kids say something like the following to "Mittie," who was half out the door but was stopped in his tracks by the cold: *"In or out, young man?"*

He'd go out but then wanted to come right back in. In the picture section of the book you'll see a classic shot of Mittie just after he went out the patio door in winter. It basically says it all.

Maybe the trout-in-the-freezer episode at a young age left him either intolerant of cold, or afraid of it, and thus, it was partially psychological. Who knows.

All I remember is that for at least five months out of the year the little guy would stare out the window, wanting to be outside, but knowing deep down it was a bad deal.

Poor little Mitten.

Poop du Jour

*We've never had a dog that ate its own poop,
or dog poop in general, but all other poop has always
been fair game for our goldens.*

There's something about dogs and poop. You can scold them until you're blue in the face and it won't make any difference. They eat poop. On our farm they eat cattle poop and horse poop. They also enjoy deer poop, although not just any deer poop. For all of our dogs, the corn- and hay-fed deer poop around our farms in east central Minnesota was always preferred over the stronger, forest-fed deer poop of northern Minnesota. It's so nice to know they have such discriminating palates.

During a day of farming, when we couldn't keep our eyes on the dogs all the time, we often paid the price that night. How fun to be in bed, invite the dogs up, and have them exhale into our faces after a few rounds of earlier pasture treats, either horse apples or cow pies.

Their all-time poopy treat is cat poop, and yes, the whole concept is pretty gross. We have gravel pads under our lean-to's on the barns, and in winter when the cats are outside up past their butts in snow, they will go under the lean-to's and do their business in the snow-free gravel. The dogs will follow, and eat cat poop. *Gross, yuck, gag, arrgh, spit-ooey.*

Of course, with four cats in the house, we have multiple litter boxes, four in fact, and *anti-dog* cat-poop management is just a part of life. We have *no* open litter boxes; they are all enclosed. One is like a kitty-litter condo, very elaborate . . . like a maze inside and totally puppy-proof. Two are covered litter boxes resembling enclosed small dog travel kennels, and one of those sits inside a large dog kennel cage with the entry door to the enclosed litter box facing in. Although all litter boxes are puppy proof, this one has to be especially safe since it is located where the dogs spend their confinement time.

This has led to something quite hilarious that has happened to both the Bors and me. The litter box in the kennel cage sits in the "dog room," that special unfinished place in our basement where we banish the dogs, and even the cats at times . . . a big mud room of sorts. To clean this litter box we have to first take it out of the kennel cage, set it on top, open it up and then get the kitty poop-scoop and poop pail. One day I was pulling the litter box out and it seemed heavier than normal. I was thinking . . . "Wow, we gotta clean this thing more often! It must be just full of poop and pee clumps." I got it out, placed it on top of the kennel cage and opened it up. There's little Naoz inside, looking somewhat bewildered.

With the Bors, it happened with Earl. We're sure both cats wondered: *whatever happened to privacy and civility?*

We blame it all on our dogs' **worst** habit . . . prowling for cat poop.

Airport welcoming committee

When you're dragging your butt off a plane,
what could be better than having your loved ones
there to welcome you?

In the post 9/11 era, the deplaning flyer can no longer be greeted at the gate. As the flyer, you have to make your way past the security checkpoint to get to your welcoming committee. Many people have found this so inconvenient that they end up being greeted at the waiting car in the chaos outside the terminal's baggage claim area.

There was a time, many years ago before the security crackdowns, when the Bors could have greeted me at the gate, but chose, instead, to greet me in the car . . . she would not go inside. The reason? *Mitten was in the car with her!* She would then drive home and I'd have the little guy right on my lap, purring away. This really was a special treat after a tiring business trip.

For many years, I thought we were the only ones crazy enough to do this little ritual, and we pretty much kept it to ourselves. But as you get to talking to good friends, stuff gets shared, and someone else has admitted to doing the same thing. NJO, another of our West Pub work pals, would get picked up after a business trip by her mom, who would have the family cat, Twinkie Marie, in the car.

Now, I'm not necessarily advocating you do this. Worst case is, perhaps your cat jumping out of the car at the airport, and you might never get it back. A dog maybe comes back, but a cat just might freak out and take off, never to be found.

That danger aside, I just thought I'd mention this as one more potentially fun thing to do with your cat or dog.

The Bors gets full credit for coming up with this little gem of kindness, not to mention her circling the airport, waiting for me to find my way out. What a champ!

Cat bagpipes
. . . and other fun things to do
with your cat, or someone else's

Our cats can be a great source of fun,
if we just give them a little help.

A cat's purr is one of the natural wonders of the world. When I'm totally stressed out, sometimes all it takes is to sit down, put my feet up, have a purring cat on my lap, and all seems right with the world. I'm no expert as to *why* they purr, but it seems they are showing contentment. You cat fanciers know purring to be a great cat feature over dogs. One of our golden retriever puppies, Nikka, sort of purred when she was a baby, but she outgrew it. Cats purr for a lifetime.

Take Pokay, who in "people years" is 118. Our wonder cat walks around purring most of the time, thinking, I'm sure, that purring, when combined with a meow, will lead to dairy products. The previously mentioned purr-meow . . . "p-u-r-r-r-e-o-w!" Very effective.

A fun time is a cat who is very anxious to eat. They will often purr while gobbling food, great fun to watch and listen to. Cats will sometimes purr while play-fighting with you, chewing on your fingers or hand, while their "motor is running." If you go too far, the purring can stop. That's the tip-off that they are ready to really put a chomp on you. For some cats, petting the guts often leads to a chomp. Scouty Pants can chomp you, pretty much out of the blue, while purring.

A purring cat reminds me of a good friend who stayed overnight at our Johnson Lake cabin with a bunch of folks from the old West-Pub-the-best-pub days. We were cramped for space so Bud slept on a mat and a sleeping bag on the floor. Early one morning, Bud woke up and was a little freaked out to find Tubby on his chest.

"Voedisch, what's this cat doing?"

"He's laying on your chest."

"No, what's that noise he's making?"

"What noise?"

"He's growling!"

I listened closely. "You nut. He's purring."

I went over to Bud and Tubby, and the cat was purring like crazy. Poor Bud. It's clear that in the nearly 50 years to that point in his life, Bud had not been a cat person.

A sleeping cat will often start purring if you just pet it gently.

For me, the highlight of purring can be demonstrated with a trick we call "cat bagpipes." Here's how it works. Cats seem to purr on both the inhale and the exhale, but it's loudest on the exhale. With the cat standing on the floor, purring away, bend over it and place your hands under its guts, sort of cradling it lightly, but with its feet still planted on the floor. Get the feel for its in-and-out purring, and try to get the timing down for the exhale. When the cat begins to do the exhale purr, *lift it off the ground quickly,* just a few inches so its feet no longer touch. What you get is an extra rush of exhaled air out of the little dickens, which causes a super loud purr. Set it back down, wait a bit and do it again.

P-u-r-o-o-o-m!

This "floor bagpipes" can become a more traditional bagpipes by carrying a purring cat, holding it under one arm. On the exhale purr, just give a squeeze on the cat with your arm, and . . . p-u-r-o-o-o-m. You can try cat bagpipes at home and, if you are gentle, you won't hurt the cat at all. If you have some concerns, "floor bagpipes" is perhaps safer than the under-the-arm approach. Thanks to our funny friend Carol for making the under-the-arm "cat bagpipes" recommendation. Why didn't we think of it?

Cat bagpipes! Try it.

OK, now that you've tried cat bagpipes, you might also enjoy "elevator butt" and "fan toes." Most cats love being patted, not petted, just in front of their tail. As you pat away, they will often push their "butt" further in the air to enhance the effect, as if on tiptoes. In fact, you can make a sitting cat, or sometimes even one that is lying down, start raising its butt and eventually rising into a standing position, just by vigorous butt patting. Don't be afraid to pat away with a little gusto; they can take it. Like "cat bagpipes," just be reasonably gentle and your cat will be fine. One of our friends has called this "elevator butt," which we think is as good a name as any.

"Fan toes" is based on a cat's instincts, kind of like always landing on its feet when falling. It works like this. Pick up the cat from behind, by placing your hands just behind its front legs, and lift it up about three feet in the air. Stop and at this point the cat is essentially hanging vertically with your grasp under its armpits, its front legs straight out with rear legs and feet pointing down. Now *slowly* lower the cat to the ground and watch its rear toes fan out, as if to give itself more stability should its feet touch the ground. Lift the cat back up and watch its rear toes retract . . . lower it down again and watch the toes fan out again. Up — retract, down — fan out.

Try this one on your friend's cat. It's possible they have never seen it before and you can pretend it's a magic trick. Something like: "You doubt my power? I'm now going to say the magic words and make your cat fan out its toes."

The magic of course is within cats themselves. Wouldn't we all be better off if we knew we would always land on our feet?

My cousin was in town and we took him and his wife out for breakfast. There was a totally strange cat on the sidewalk and I asked them if they had ever seen "cat fan toes." They had to admit they had not, and seemed skeptical when I described it. I bent down and petted the cat to be sure it was socially OK, picked it under its front legs and proceeded to demonstrate perfect fan toes. They were a bit amazed.

Now, there you are. Three things to do with a cat, not necessarily your own, on a rainy day: "cat bagpipes," "elevator butt" and "fan toes." Now, aren't you fortunate to be reading this book?

Mitten was excellent at all three. Today Earl Gray gets the nod for cat bagpipes, and all of our current cats perform well doing elevator butt and fan toes.

Except Pokay. She was issued her *get-out-of-stunts-free* pass long ago, and has retired as the undisputed champ of cat bagpipes. She still purrs like crazy.

Note: There's another fun cat feature, not something you can do with a cat, but something cats can have, or not have. We call it "marionette chops." If a cat's under-chin is a different color than the rest of its face, and you look at the cat's head from underneath, we think it looks like a marionette's mouth. A ventriloquist's dummy might have the same look. Calico Scouty has a whitish face but under her chin she is all black, an excellent marionette combination.

Pokay has a blackish face with a tan under-chin. What really sets her apart is that she will sometimes open her mouth to meow, and nothing will come out. If she continues in this way, you can provide her with a meow of your own, like a ventriloquist.

Mitten had no marionette chops, nor did he ever swallow his meow. In some ways he was just an average cat, but you'd never hear him admit it.

Recording a cat

If a movie cartoon fire truck or police car needed a siren,
sometimes it would be a cat tied to the fender,
with some cartoon guy stretching out the window,
cranking the cat's tail. The implication was
that a cat's meow is pretty awful. I find cat sounds
quite neat and certainly worth sharing, even recording.

We are a musical bunch of sorts. It's not that we play a lot of instruments; it's just that we really like music. I introduced Bors and the kids to classical stuff and some old rock and roll. Bors liked her Fogelberg and Springsteen from college. But it was really Robbie who, by about age 8, became a music maven in the making. He started to create tapes from any source he could find — FM radio, records, other tapes. It wasn't long before he became a little storehouse of trivia, like what bass player was in this or that group, and when. And his tastes ran true, at least in our book. He would record 10,000 Maniacs, REM, U2, Crowded House, Robbie Robertson, the Police and later, Sting.

Rob taught himself to play guitar and then bass guitar. In his Seattle U-dub graduate school days, he formed a band, wrote some music and they made a CD. It's the first disc in our system's CD changer . . . *Sons of Norway.*

Amy plays piano and she gets her grandmother's Everett whenever she has room. For now it's with us but neither the Bors nor I can do much with it. Sometimes the cats will walk on it if the keyboard is open, especially Naoz.

Early on, I gave Bors, Punky and Amertile this riddle of my own creation:

Me: You know the rock group *Bread*?

Them: Yah?

Me: They're toast.

The ungrateful slugs just groaned. How cruel.

In the early '80s we had a very good stereo system as well as multiple boom boxes. We only had a turntable and tape deck since music CDs were just a bright idea back then. Both the stereo and the boom boxes had microphones so we could be our own "DJs," introducing the songs we would record on tape, or just do our own singing and recording. Sometimes we would do comedy tapes of ourselves . . . just funny stuff.

One night I was fooling around, trying to get the Bors to say some stuff on tape. She refused, despite my efforts, but I've got her refusals on tape. I tried begging, tickling, even dragging her around on the carpet over to the mike. No dice.

Mitten walked through, purring up a storm, and I thought: why battle with the un-cooperative Bors when I have a willing recording subject right here? Mitten!

It was pretty easy, really. I just tried to create the conditions where the little goof made neat and funny noises, then recorded him. Of course, any of the following would have worked nicely: purring while eating, cat bagpipes, purring while chomping on my hand as I tickled his tummy, the impromptu meow-purr, the nursing station purr . . . whatever he felt like doing or whatever worked. However, that particular night his regular old basic purr was so loud, it was all I really needed, along with him actually rubbing the microphone with his whiskers while purring.

As I recorded him, he just kept on purring like crazy, louder and louder actually. I played it back and howled. Mitten heard the playback and looked a little terrified. Try it with your cat. I don't know if you'll get too much from a dog, unless you can get them to bark, growl or whine. But when you start with the basic purring cat and then try for the purr-variations outlined here and elsewhere in the book, you really can't miss.

I still have Mitten on tape, which is a special treasure. Our good friend Ray from Utah, who had a cat, "The Judge," for over 20 years, loves this tape.

"MITT-en!"

In the middle of a book on Mitten is a chapter called "MITT-en!" "How come?" you ask. Maybe the best way to explain this is to say that the little guy's grip has transcended logic and time.

Little "Mittie" was mostly a homebody, spending far more time in than out. I would be wandering the house and there he'd be, lying on a chair, couch or bed, or following me, meowing for something, or for no reason whatsoever. He usually just seemed to be somewhere close at hand.

Our family has always talked to our pets, perhaps bordering on the unhealthy. The first thing we do when we see one of our kitties or pups is to acknowledge them by calling their name. It makes no difference that we just saw them five minutes earlier in another room; if we run into them again, it's . . . "Baby Bails," "Oh, hi Pokay," "Scouty Pants," "Aw, Naoz," "Nikka-pup."

These acknowledgments are nothing compared to the rather loud "MITT-en!" that Bors and I used when we saw his highness. The "MITT" part was high up, almost a gravel-voiced yell, which would tail off to the more subdued "-en." "MITT-en!"

What happened, however, is that we would start barking his name whether he was around *or not*. Family and friends, like sister Meg (Maggie), would sometimes do the "MITT-en" bark whenever they saw him. But the spontaneous "MITT-en," with no Mitten in sight, was reserved for the Bors and me. It became sort of a house cheer or whatever.

But it gets nuttier. We eventually started using "Mitten" as our generic term for "cat." We'd be driving in the car, see a cat slinking in the roadside ditch or in someone's front yard, and out it would come . . . "MITT-en!" Watching a movie on the tube and a cat is in the picture . . . "MITT-en!" To this day, that's what we say when we see a cat.

Finally, and this is where you will think we've slid off the summit a bit, it's nearly eight years after his passing and we still walk around the house and yell "MITT-en" for absolutely no reason whatsoever. I have characterized this as the *Moby Dick Effect* — "You'll bark Mitten where there be no Mitten."

Molly and Rob have been together for several years, but Molly has never known Mitten. The first time Rob brought Molly to the farm, she apparently asked him on the way home . . . "Why does your dad yell 'Mitten' around the house?" She thought I had some kind of nervous disorder.

I guess the little whiskered nut is still in charge.

Watch dogs?

*The horse barn, lots of visitors, riding horses, vehicles coming
and going, hustle and bustle, and barking goldens! . . .
Mitten would not have been thrilled
with one of the things we are doing at the farm today.*

O ur goldens have always been sort of watchdog types, but only
halfway. They'll bark like crazy when a car drives up, but if a
burglar ever came in the house, Bailey would offer to carry his
toolkit, and Nikka would follow after with a toy in her mouth,
waiting for the thief to play with her.

We operate a therapy horseback riding program for disabled
kids and adults. With the Bors as our site's NAHRA certified
therapy instructor, we work with a non-profit called *We Can Ride,*
based in the western suburbs of Minneapolis, in Minnetonka. *We
Can Ride* provides us with the client riders, as well as donated

horses, since our own herd does not have enough good therapy riding steeds. It generally takes a lead person and two side-walkers for each horse and rider combination, thus volunteers are crucial to the success of the program. On Wednesday nights, in eight week sessions each spring, summer and fall, we hold two classes, one starting at 6:30 p.m. and one at 7:45. Volunteers come early to get the horses tacked-up and ready, and they stay late to put the horses away, return the tack and generally help put the place back into shape. Our volunteers are the best.

At any point in time on Wednesday evenings, there could be four or more vehicles near the horse barn and arena area, vehicles that brought the riders and their parents or caregivers, and another dozen or more vehicles belonging to volunteers, parked further away. The puppies go wild, barking like crazy as each new car pulls in. They calm down, but only until the next car shows up. They just can't help it. We can't do anything about it, of course, because we are down in the barn while the pups are banished to the house. Our visitors can hear the barking, and many folks wish the pups could join us.

What the puppies really want, of course, is to visit everyone. The more folks they can meet and mooch affection off of, the better. They just seem so puzzled as to why mom and dad won't take them down to meet and greet.

The treat comes the last night of each session. I volunteer with a rider I'll call Tim, who is blind and has some other challenges. One of the nicest guys you'll ever meet, Tim really loves dogs, yet we feel it would just add to the chaos if Bailey and Nikka were down at the horse barn and arena during classes, even if leashed or confined. Even Callie Kitty, our current barn cat, gets locked in a kennel until class is over. But at the end of the last night of each eight-week session, when everyone is filing out, I go up to the house, put the excited pups on leashes, and bring them down to meet Tim and anyone who wants to stay behind and greet these truly wonderful characters. After some initial excitement, they are calm and wolfing the affection that just naturally comes their way.

Our pups just don't get it, I'm sure. They were born to be with people, and this house-banishment baloney makes zero sense in their minds.

Tim will often ask, "Are the puppies coming down tonight?" How fun for me when I can finally say, "Yes, Tim, tonight's the night."

If Mitten were alive, on therapy riding nights he would ignore the whole thing.

"Get up, you slugs."

Pets have all sorts of ways of telling you it's time to get up.
Some of these can be less than funny to the dozing human.

Our dogs and cats have always spent nights in our bedroom. We were never ones to banish the little characters to the kitchen or basement. They are part of the family and we shall all sleep together. The problem comes when the sleep schedules get out of synch and they decide it's time to get up when you've got another 37 winks in the hopper.

The relatively easy stuff is the in-and-out business that just happens. A cat wants to go out at 2 a.m. and come back in at 4:30. Or the pups need to pee in the middle of the night. Oh sure, it's a pain in the ass, but at least I know I'm heading back to the fart sack and the land of Winkin' and Blinkin', assuming I can doze off again.

The really bum times are when a pet thinks it's time to start the day, and Bors and I disagree. They have such interesting and sometimes totally annoying ways of getting us up, and Mitten was by far the most creative, and most annoying.

Pokay is pretty tame. To this day her wake-up routine is still the same. She comes up on the bed about 6 a.m., does a few head butts and then starts to purr, very loudly. If we show no signs of waking, she will go up on the low, flat headboard affair, sit there and just purr away. It's so loud that if we wake for any reason, that's pretty much it; her purring will keep you awake. She will sit and purr for a half hour or more.

Scouty and Earl will walk on me, as does Nikka, which can be a real discomfort. But Nikka takes it up a notch by actually lying on top of us. Uff. Bailey will lick my face, normally a fun thing, but it can be very confusing, depending on what I might be dreaming about at the moment.

Mitten was the champ wake-up artist. At the old farm we had a tall headboard deal, another flat top design, that is now in our guest room. I was dozing away and the little grunt climbed on top of the headboard, and executed a swan dive right onto my unsuspecting guts. After a severe scolding, I tossed him outside by the scruff of his neck. He never did it again.

He had three other methods of getting us up that were much less severe, but very effective. To get just me up he would start the nursing thing. He just never nursed on the Bors. Scouty Pants does the same thing today, but she'll nurse on either of us.

Mitten employed two other methods that worked on both the Bors and I. One was to race across the bed at top speed. He was

100

so fast I could not catch him, so I had no choice but to get up and either throw him out, follow him to his food dish for a small feeding, or lock him up somewhere. The Bors always said, never reward bad behavior with food.

In his declining years he graduated to the energy-conserving "newspaper flip." If a section of newspaper was on the floor next to the bed, he would just sit there and flip it with his paw, over and over again, until one of us stirred.

Clever fellow, this Mitten.

Scouty Pants has given the newspaper thing a twist. She will sit on the floor and shred the newspaper, chewing pieces off, spitting them out and chewing some more. This is a two-fold pain since after we get up, we then have a mess to clean up. Grrr.

Pokay the wonder cat

Pokay has lived well beyond 20, but she could have been toast at 8 weeks of age. It was all pretty much the luck of the draw.

There is a cultural difference between parts of our family when it comes to how pets are managed. For example, when a new pet arrives at our place, either by design or as a stray, and it is going to stay, one of the early tasks is reproductive surgery. To us, it makes sense to do this for many reasons, which I won't bore you with here. (Editor Pat thinks this will be covered in my next book. *Next book?*) As Township Chairman, I have had to tell folks who call that our animal control officer will handle dog situations, but not cats. There are just too many cats roaming the countryside, primarily because folks won't spend the time and money to get them fixed. Whether male or female, in our view it's the right thing to do for both cats and dogs.

On Laurie's side of the family, in the small town and farming area of rural east central Minnesota, fixing a cat is sometimes seen as too expensive or too much of a bother, or whatever, so there has been litter after litter on the family farm, for decades. Some of the farm kittens get placed of course, and if needed, maybe one is kept with the mother on the farm as an extra "mouser." But those who survive and don't find a home may meet an untimely demise. I'm not saying anyone is right or wrong here; we just do things differently.

Curled up again on a pad next to me as I type away is Pokay, the ageless wonder. She arrived in April of 1984, along with littermate Tubby, from Bors' family farm. It was the introduction of these two cuties that put Mitten's little nose out of joint for quite a long time. I'm sure his plans were to remain an only child, but alas, Bors' mission to rescue two of the farm kitties ruined everything. They would chase Mitten around, sending him up on top of chair backs and other furniture, to then look down and growl. I have to believe that those growls were half meant for us.

Tubby croaked fairly early in life, at age 9, hit by a car out in front of our first farm. He just had this bug up his butt to wander that none of our other pets ever had. Our first farm was 21 acres, smaller than our current farm just a half mile away, but plenty of land to roam around on. But it was not enough for our Tubby.

His sister, Pokay, has always been much more the stay-at-home type, never straying at all, except for her famous Johnson Lake adventure. But it wasn't just cautious living that added years to her life, because once a cat reaches 15 or so, you know there are some solid built-in genes at work.

When Pokay was perhaps 17, we noticed that she would walk around the kitchen and howl for food, even though she was still eating two squares a day at her feeding station on the basement workbench. There didn't have to be anything cooking or even out on the counter giving off an aroma. She just knew what the fridge was all about, and that it always contained *dairy products*. These are her passion and her savior I suppose, for it was then that I began feeding her dairy products, the occasional leftover chicken or whatever was in the fridge, several times a day. It was pretty easy really . . . just take some half and half, whipping cream, sour cream, cheese, cream cheese, or ice cream . . . plop a little on her "kitchen dish," and watch her go at it. Even a shot of 1% milk would do the trick, although I knew she needed calories, so low-fat milk was not her usual treat.

We've kept up this supplemental feeding for nearly seven years and she's still with us. Now, we have to do two additional things for this system to work. First, dairy products are light in color and in deference to Pokay's aging eyes, we serve her on a dark blue saucer so she can see what's going on. Second, we have to make sure that other pets, especially the goldens, let her finish. Their treat is to lick up what she leaves, but *not* until she is done.

We've heard that a cat's life in human years is 5 to 1, so she would be about 118. She's old, slow and has to be picked up gently. But she purrs up a storm, loves to be combed, gives you the loving head butts only cats can give, and still has the energy to swat a dog on the nose, or put Scouty or Earl Gray, our newest cats, in their place.

She is getting pretty thin, however, thus her newest name, "Little Po."

She has since hopped to the floor, wandered to the kitchen and is yeowling for dairy products right now.

"I'm coming, Pokay."

Speaking of age, if you're getting a little long in the tooth like me, have you ever heard an old, easy-listening instrumental on radio and wondered: "Now, is this Acker Bilk, Bent Fabric, Bert Kaempfert or Horst Jankowski?"

The golden bond

Looking for the perfect dog? Try a golden retriever.

Bors bonds with her horses, but I generally don't. Maggie was the exception; she was my special horse. I raised her from birth, having her in a halter on her second day of life, much to her mother's puzzlement and the Bors' consternation. While I was retired and stealing Maggie's childhood affections, Bors was still in her career at West-Pub-the-Best-Pub, and I had the freedom to do the early training and thus, the early bonding.

Maggie suffered a bad ankle wound early in life and eight years later we lost her to a recurring infection in that same ankle. One regret we had was never breeding her. The staff at the U of M equine hospital were crying their eyes out when we gave the OK to put her down. Laurie and I sobbed most of the way home.

Someone once asked me what was so special about Maggie. I responded that she was the most golden retriever-like horse I had ever known. She would actually give me hugs with her head and neck. She was a big horse, a Friesen-Thoroughbred cross, and she would have to lean down to do her "hug." And like a golden, she had the most kind eyes, kinder than any horse we have known.

Our golden retrievers, what we consider to be the best all-around dog breed, have brought us so much joy and completeness. Energetic, smart, playful, loving and completely loyal, they are kind to children and other animals. What more could you ask of a dog? OK, maybe a little less shedding hair would be nice.

When we met our current breeder and she asked what we were looking for, I said . . . "a young man, a cross between Einstein and Red Skelton." Nancy knew exactly what we meant.

Nancy is a very diligent breeder, not only in how she manages her bloodline, but in how she places her dogs. When we were first referred to her, she started with a phone interview of *us*, and it was only when *we* passed her muster, that she sent us an application. To the completed application we attached a cover letter and pictures of our farm and of our goldens, Kirby and Katie, even though Kirby had passed away. We passed that test and only then did she invite us to her farm in Wisconsin where she could size us up in person, and also have us meet her *nine adult goldens,* including one very sweet girl ready to deliver.

Nancy does something I'll just call controlled puppy placement. After all the interviews and discussions of what we were looking for in a puppy, she made it very clear that **she** *places the* *dog with the owner . . .* **we don't pick our puppy.** This may sound a little overboard, but it works. After two visits to the first litter with her, we found ourselves falling in love with a puppy which, of course, she warned us not to do. But by week seven this little guy had a personality shift that we could not witness, and he became very quiet and somewhat reclusive.

We had only seen this puppy and his littermates for two visits of an hour each, once at week three (no handling) and once at week six, after their shots, when we could handle them. As Nancy explained, all it takes is for a puppy to have an "off" day during one of our visits and we would never know that it might be the gem of the litter for us. At week seven, another young fellow, whom we really had not noticed, blossomed.

When Nancy told us on the phone of her decision to place the unknown little "Brow" with us and assign *our* "Butt Boy" to someone else, we were not happy at all. Our "Butt Boy" was already gone, but we drove over anyway. We were half expecting to just ask for our down payment back; we were not in a good mood. But when we saw "Brow," a little guy with a very pronounced forehead, all by himself, we were toast. He is our beloved Bailey. The, by then, somewhat reclusive "Butt Boy" ended up with a family with a small boy who wasn't ready for a real energy-loaded puppy.

Nancy's placements made for the best result all around, and you don't get this when buyers do the picking.

Our little Nikka also came from Nancy's wonderful farm, as well as three other goldens placed with families we referred to Nancy. Two of them, Syd (a female) and Jack, often come to stay at our farm when their "mom," our very good friend MC, takes a trip. Thank goodness Bailey likes to sleep on the cold floor or it would be *four* goldens on the bed at one time while we are trying to sleep. Three is plenty, and tends to keep the cat count down at night. Animals on the bed at night are generally fine unless (a) they start taking up serious room, or (b) they start heating things up.

What a zoo.

You've never had a puppy and now you think you might want one? MC made the following observation about puppies. For the first few months, puppies are far more work than babies. At least babies don't move around much and you have a more or less systematic way of handling their output. Puppies are tearing around from the moment they come home from the breeder, pooping and peeing anytime and anywhere, with no diapers or other output management system. MC makes a strong case.

Every time we bring a new one home we remember all over again how much work it can be. Most recently, we cared for a puppy from Hearing and Service Dogs of Minnesota for over a month. He had just come from the breeder and after a week at the HSDM kennel, he came to us at about nine weeks of age. We cared for him until he could be placed with his first-level trainer. One word . . . "Whew!"

Our first goldens, Kirby and Katie, came from more or less backyard breeders. This is, I'm sure, how many folks find a puppy, either word of mouth or following the classifieds to find generally well-meaning folks who just want a litter of pups. You can have great success going this route. We sure did.

Kirby came to us in 1988. Many male puppies in Minnesota got the tag "Kirby" back then, in honor of Kirby Puckett, the recently deceased Hall of Fame baseball player for the Minnesota Twins, who led the hometown team to two World Series championships in 1987 and 1991. At the ballpark, Bob Casey, the venerable stadium announcer, would introduce the players coming to bat. For the "Puck," he would call . . . "and batting third, Kirb-eeeeee Puck-ett!" When you named your dog Kirby, you could do the same thing in your backyard. Something like . . . "And here he comes, Kirb-eeeeee Pupp-y!"

OK, just a goofy Minnesota thing, I guess, but it repeated itself all over the state in those days.

When our Kirby died, Katie was just in a funk, but unlike us, she was not pulling out of it very well. How could she know what happened? Who comforts her? Kirby bonded to us but Katie mostly bonded to Kirby. He was pretty much the delight of her life, and when he left her, her eyes were so sad. She spent long hours looking out the patio doors and windows. We were sure she was just waiting for him to return. She would sometimes just lie in the backyard, head erect, staring out toward the wetland and hills beyond, where they had gone on their great adventures together. She would sit, watch and wait. We were so sad for her and just tried to keep her busy as best we could.

Her eventual tonic was little Bailey.

Our very good friend, the Z, has had little black cockapoos for many years. His latest was also a Kirby. We were still at the old farm and Z was heading up north with his family, and needed someone to take care of his Kirby for the weekend.

We couldn't count the number of dogs we have cared for while their owners took a trip or whatever. We are no fans of commercial care kennels ourselves; in fact, we have *never* used one. So if you're a good friend of ours and your dog gets along with our dogs and cats, and can be convinced not to chase cattle or eat horse apples, and we are home anyway, we will puppy-sit. So over came Z's Kirby, but of course we had to be careful to *never use his name around Katie.*

Our primary precaution when taking care of someone else's dog is to place a tag on the collar right away, with just our phone number on it. If the visiting hound ever does flee, and we can't find it, we would rely on this tag to help us get it back. Thankfully, we've never lost one, but we've had two scares. We were all outside on the Saturday we had Z's dog, and for whatever reason, little Kirby took off to the back of the farm on his own, out of sight. Katie and baby Bailey never budged.

It's that sinking feeling we have had just twice over the years: *we lost someone else's dog.* Ugh. So we started the search and, somewhat desperately, and without thinking, I gave a loud "Kirrr-beeeee!" Katie immediately sat up, her eyes frozen on the wetland and hills beyond, eagerly watching, waiting, hoping. Laurie's tears flowed like rain as she noticed Katie sitting at attention, watching. Then it was my turn to sob. We were so sad for our little girl. We went over and just gave her huge hugs and tried to direct her attention elsewhere.

In the meantime, my calling worked, and back the little visitor came.

You dread the loss of your pets. As with our Kirby, we expect Bailey to go first and at that point, we will not only have to prop up each other, but also Nikkapup, who will be sad and lonely for sure.

Such is our bond with our goldens, and they with each other.

Later, you will learn of our experiences with cancer, and how we have lost three dogs to this disease. Katie was from a litter of eleven, and at age 12, she outlived all of her littermates. The exception to the relatively short lives of goldens these days was Papa, named after Papageno, the bird catcher from Mozart's opera *The Magic Flute*. Papa sometimes stayed with us when his family, SLH and Patricia, went on vacation. He would arrive with his golden pal, Sophie, named after a character in *Der Rosenkavalier*. We have never had a golden come to stay who has misbehaved in any major way, and all have gotten along with our dogs. They do have to pass a preliminary "cat test" however, especially if they are not accustomed to having cats around.

Papa passed away in the spring of 2007 at age 16½, the longest living golden of any we have known.

We do open our home to dogs other than goldens. Jen and Dave will drop off their huge Bernese mountain dog, and Walter Batman does just fine with our dogs. He was a little too curious about our cats at first, but he's learning. We have also cared for two shelties, Pogo and Jet, pups of our very good friends JWA and KMA, although Jet seems to have my number.

Before we take a dog we just ask that they bring their pup over for a visit first to see how well things go. The shelties also needed some training about the cats, and then they were fine. We would much rather take care of a dog than have the owner farm it out to a kennel, where, frankly, some bad things can happen.

Papa had to have his tail docked after he came back from an extended kennel stay. His family suspected the kennel operator shut a cage door on Papa's tail. The tail bone was broken, an infection developed, and part of the tail had to be removed. A golden retriever with a bobbed tail; what a bad deal. No lost tails on our watch.

Another golden we know, Murphy, was at a kennel while his family was on vacation. They had their laptop computer along and they could access the kennel's web site, view the kennel's play-room cam, and see firsthand how Murphy was doing. Imagine their *horror* when they viewed a huge dog holding Murphy by the back of the neck, pinning him to the floor. They called the kennel immediately and chewed them out royally. No one at the kennel was watching the playroom. Duh.

I'm sure lots of folks have good experiences with boarding kennels, but it's just not something we are ever going to do. When we are gone, we need a "farm sitter" anyway to take care of the cattle and horses, so adding our dogs and cats to the assignment is not too difficult.

I offer this final plug for the golden retriever. They are exceptional service dogs, adept at search and rescue, whether in earthquake rubble or an avalanche. As a helpmate to humans, they are a preferred breed for Hearing and Service Dogs of Minnesota (HSDM). Very trainable and eager to please, they can assist the physically impaired, including the hearing-challenged. Our very good friend, Alicia, has dealt with MS for many years, and now has a golden retriever service dog, Tanner, from HSDM. When she and her husband take a rare trip without Tanner, he comes to stay with us and is just a delight.

Vitamin hockey

Cats can be very athletic. Mitten boxed,
and Miss Scouty Pants plays hockey.

Cats get extra nutty in the kitchen. The fridge (and in Mitten's case, the freezer as well) holds an extra attraction for the little gremlins. Food smells seem to be the ticket. I can remember my mother's reaction when Buttons would lay right behind her at the sink, waiting for some food to hit the floor. She'd turn around and nearly fall over the cat almost every time, with "Damn cat!" following from her otherwise usually civil tongue.

It was the kitchen table and counters that really bugged her. Sometimes Buttons just couldn't stay off, looking for crumbs, the butter dish or whatever he could find. I've found this to be true with nearly every cat I've ever known . . . a fondness for going up on kitchen counters. You know they can learn not to, and you know *they know* they shouldn't. But some will just do it anyway.

Our latest knucklehead in this regard is Little Miss Scouty Pants. She has a really crazy reason for going up on counters; besides food, she is looking for loose vitamins. She likes to play *vitamin hockey*.

She also likes "Chubby Chuck," our name for a protein shake made with banana, milk and protein powder, half vanilla, half chocolate. Once the blender starts she can hardly stand it because she knows that when the noise is done she will actually get some. I turn the top of the blender upside down on a saucer on the floor and she attacks it as if she hasn't eaten in a week. The dogs wait for her to finish so they can get in their licks.

Why "Chubby Chuck?" If you remember the movie *American Graffiti,* you may recall "the Toad" borrowing the car, then going to the drive-in and ordering a classic meal of American cinema: "I'll have a Double Chubby Chuck, fries and a Coke." Laurie and I have been using the protein shake as a way of getting nutrition without a huge breakfast meal, which might help keep our weight in check, thus "Chubby Chuck." You will sometimes hear this more sophisticated name around the house: "How about a round of Rotund Charles?" It's like our family name for Sloppy Joes: the "Untidy Joseph."

Anyway, that's Scouty's morning snack. But her morning treat is to play vitamin hockey. It goes like this. Scouty Pants (Scouty) knows that morning means vitamins, and there she is, bright and early, looking for her opportunity. She hops up on the "Chubby" counter, illegally of course, and any vitamins or pills that have been set out but not yet consumed, she swats to the floor, jumps down and proceeds to bat them all over the hardwoods.

Vitamin hockey. It seems quite Mitten-like, but Scouty is the only cat to actually do it. Our job is to immediately pick this stuff up, lest Bailey snarfs up 5 mg. of Lipitor, some fish oil, baby aspirin, mega-vitamins, Lutein or calcium.

Vitamin hockey . . . what else would a Minnesota cat play?

The family Christmas photo

Each year we include a family photo with our Christmas card. It would be so much easier if there were just people involved.

Early in the proceedings, Bors and I decided to start a tradition of taking a family photo to include with our Christmas card. From the very beginning we thought the pets should be a part of the deal. This decision has added time, sometimes frustration, and I must admit, a whole lot of fun to the process. It has also made for a much more interesting end result.

Kirby arrived in 1988 and Katie in 1990, so in the early years of 1986–87 we had just the cats — Mitten, Tubby and Pokay. Laurie would set up the camera on a tripod, frame up the shot, set it for a delayed shutter, then dash back to the huddle. I would often hold the somewhat annoyed Mitten, and he rarely looked like he was having a good time. After the dogs arrived, we had to manage five animals between four people: me, the Bors, Robbie and Amy. Someone was stuck managing two, and Bors had to hurry back and secure her animal before the flash. This generally took many shots since this was pre-digital and you just never knew what you were going to get.

It was organized mayhem.

For the past several years it has just been the Bors and me so we have generally left the cats out of it, the pups being easier to manage. Some of these Christmas card photos can be found in the photo section of this book.

It's been fun to travel around visiting friends and relatives and seeing our Christmas picture still under a refrigerator magnet in January . . . or June.

I got extra mileage from some of these shots, those where I would be holding the Mitten, and we actually caught him facing the camera, even if he did look like Mr. Grumpy Pants, or when I was securing a dog who didn't look totally spaced out. From time to time, I've had to submit a personal photo for a special photo ID, such as my Professional Association of Diving Instructors (PADI) scuba dive card, or the season lift pass at the local ski hill. I took a copy of the annual Christmas photo, cut out me and Katie, and sent it along to PADI so they could make my photo ID card. Sure enough, back came the photo ID with me *and Katie,* right there on the ID card.

When I show the card, the dive master might say something like "Hey, cute. Your dog's in the photo," to which I would respond, "Of course, she and I got scuba certified together."

Then there's Bailey and me on one of my annual local ski passes, which would hang right on my ski jacket. "He stayed home today with the sniffles; otherwise, he'd be out on the slopes with me right now. The season pass covers both of us, you know."

I did an ID with a photo of me and the Mitten, but it's lost. Thus the only photo ID examples in the photo section of this book are the two mentioned above.

Just a dumb thing to do, I suppose, that some folks have enjoyed.

I find a family picture, with or without pets, more interesting than the long holiday letters. Oh, oh. I wonder who might read this and subsequently stop sending us their holiday letter, or any greeting whatsoever. Ooops.

Mother Katie

Mitten's biggest pain in the butt was any small puppy.
He had some success swatting a kitten into its place,
and even larger dogs, but puppies never seemed to get the hint.
We never did apologize to him for Katie's puppies.

We now believe that dog breeding should be a serious undertaking, done only by people who know what they're doing, and for the right reasons, like the improvement of the breed. Like many well-intentioned folks, we thought we would "try it" once since we just loved puppies so much. Our mother would be Katie and we held off getting her fixed so we could try a breeding sometime in her third year. The father was also a golden, "Norman," owned by a West co-worker.

Talk about novices. We brought Norman home when Katie was coming into heat, but he had no clue what to do. He had the tools but, apparently, *no manual.* The Bors came up with the idea of locking them both up in a horse stall and just let them be for an hour or so. We tried various other routines for a couple of days before we took Norman home. Since we were not able to watch them every minute, we had no idea if they "did the deed" or not. For sure, nothing much happened when we were watching.

After a few weeks, Katie started looking a little heavy, so we took her in for a pregnancy check and, sure enough, she was "with pups." We set up a special whelping pen under the basement steps. It was nothing fancy, just enclosed on three sides with slats. A short board on the front let Katie get out for potty trips but the pups would still be confined. With lots of bedding and a heat lamp, we were all set. We would add newspapers for "puppy potties" once they were born.

When the time came, we were ready, even if Katie wasn't. I have never seen a dog in so much misery. She just seemed like she was going to die for maybe 24 hours. She probably wanted to be on our soft bed for comfort but we knew she had to stay downstairs and not deliver her brood just anywhere in the house. The night she delivered she seemed to understand what the whelping pen was for, and in she went. After a lot of work and constant panting, out came one, and in a few minutes, another. Bors went upstairs for the video camera but when she got back, Katie was relaxed, cleaning her two puppies. And that was that.

The golden litters we have known have been 6 to 12 puppies, so naturally we expected many more. We had a waiting list of folks ten deep who wanted a puppy, but no additional puppies came. We went to bed and hoped for more, but at 6 a.m., there she was, looking happy as a clam with her *two* little ones. *Litter? Two??* There were many disappointed people at work that day.

Not wanting to get too attached, we called one "Brownie" because she had a brown tummy, and the other one we called "Standard" since she had a regular light-colored tummy. But we grew to love them dearly, and they were so much fun. Kirby took great pride as if they were his own. He played with them a lot and "showed them the ropes." He was so patient when one had him by the ear and the other had him by the tail. But if the baby needle teeth got to be too much, a very deep growl and a curl of his lip were in store, and they snapped to attention and immediately behaved . . . until they did it all over again.

And they really bugged the Mitten. At that time we had a single household litter box that was in the basement, so Mitten and the other cats had to run the puppy gauntlet just to do their business. I don't recall but Mitten probably spent more time than normal outside during those eight weeks when the puppies ran the show.

They grew like weeds. Having their choice of many milk spigots, they soon became healthy little butterballs.

"Brownie girl" went to Bors' cousin's family in Wisconsin and "Standard girl" went to MC's sister in Omaha.

It was a great experience and such a delight, but we were really crushed when they had to go to their new homes. Even Rob and Amy were sad. That was it. We were done. We decided to leave breeding to the professionals and never send the Mitten through that particular torture again.

Dying without dignity

If you are treating your dog for cancer with weekly chemotherapy treatments, in addition to who is treating your dog and at what facility, it may be even more important what day of the week your dog is getting treatments.

Death with dignity is a goal that can be elusive and, sometimes, just not possible. We can do more for our pets in this regard than we can for family members. Death with dignity was elusive for Dad, and for Kirby.

We all thought Dad would die of heart failure. After his doozie of a coronary, the 1952 "Buttons" heart attack, and three later, less severe, episodes, he eventually succumbed to lung cancer in 1980 at the age of 77. When I once asked him, he said he started smoking at Wentworth Military Academy in Missouri at age 15. He carried on right through his Naval Academy days, the Universities of North Dakota and Wisconsin, the Depression, marriage, family, career — never quitting, ever. Sixty two years of smoking. *Good thing he switched to filters in 1952.*

We couldn't afford in-home care for Dad, and Mom said she was not strong enough to care for him, so into a nursing home he went, to die. Sadly, it took another five months or more, longer than the doctors thought it would take. What a lousy way for Dad to go.

I would visit, often bringing the grandkids, Robbie and Amy. These were good visits but were rather hard on the kids. On visits by myself, a little gin rummy or cribbage was sometimes in order. It was always so good to be with him, but these were not fun visits as I saw him slowly fade away.

His oncologist said Dad should lay off the smokes at this point, something about adding to the irritation and pain in his lungs or whatever. Dad's attitude was . . . what . . . is he nuts? I'm dying, for crapsakes. What harm can smoking do now?

Dad just liked people, and he made friends early at the nursing home. He would stash his heaters with the orderlies and they would bring him his smokes one at a time, just a few each day. We learned that Dad had his last smoke the day before he died.

The way Dad wasted away in a nursing home with terminal cancer is not my idea of dying with dignity. Today, we would have considered a hospice approach, perhaps even at home.

With our pets, we can do better. When we "put Buster down" or "put Muffin to sleep," we are taking their lives in our hands, making the terribly difficult decision that their suffering exceeds any joy they may have in living . . . and if we can do this while not letting our own fear of losing them get in the way, we can help them end their lives mercifully and with dignity. It's an amazing blessing, really, and a heavy responsibility.

When you get your kitten or puppy you also get the responsibility of *helping them end their lives.* Sorry, folks, that's the way it is, or should be. Are you as disgusted as I am about the cheesy and bullshit reasons people give for giving up their pets? As pets age they can become somewhat inconvenient in their feeding, potty habits, shedding, and veterinary needs. So what? Pets should be for a lifetime, not like some piece of furniture you discard when you no longer want it around. Don't get me started on some of the crap-ola reasons I've heard people give for trucking their pets to the animal shelter, or for putting them down, their *reasons of inconvenience.*

Cancer seems to be the curse of the dog world right now. For something that's not contagious, it's almost an epidemic. The kids' first dog was a Sheltie named "CJ" who got hit by the school bus before he was even a year old. Devastating. The kids did not see CJ being buried, so they never got to say goodbye. Protecting a child from the harsh realities of the death of a pet is not always the best course. We picked up Robbie and Amy as usual on Friday, the day after CJ was hit by the school bus. Amy was sobbing all over again and Laurie held her all the way up to the cabin. When we got there Amy and Laurie went for a potty break and, oddly, found a little dead kitty at the door of the outhouse. They talked about what to do and decided it needed to be buried. Laurie recounts how they even said a little prayer. In some related way, Amy was much better almost immediately about CJ, and stopped sobbing.

The family around the corner had a female Sheltie they had bred, and they promised our kids the pick of the litter. Muffy was born a few weeks later and it was immediately clear that this "purebred Sheltie" litter was a little off-key . . . the two pups she delivered had, like, zero legs, just little shorties like a Dachshund. The father of this litter was no Sheltie, but the two puppies were darling. Muffy soon became the kids' dog of a lifetime. Going with us to the lake every weekend, she was always a total delight.

Muffy had this stunt of coming up to anyone in a chair and lifting her hind leg straight out in back while standing right next to the foot of the person's top crossed leg. One of our cabin visitors, our good friend NJO, was convinced Muffy was about to pee on her when, in fact, all she wanted was for NJO to rub her guts with her foot. We would just howl when she did this to someone new. This was Muffy's "gut-rub ballet."

She also learned a fun trick. The cue was "dead" and she would fall over. The trick was then shown to anyone new. It went like this: "Muffy, what would you rather do, be married or be *dead*?" . . . and she'd fall over. Hilarious. Try it. It's an easy one to teach, and a treat for your guests. Our friend Bud, the one who didn't know what a cat's purr was, taught our family this puppy trick. Thanks, Bud.

Muffy contracted lymphatic cancer at age 9, pretty young, we thought, for a small dog. This cancer can be hard to detect and, in fact, someone else who was visiting the farm and was playing with her, first felt the small lump on the back of one of Muffy's hind legs. We gave the fluffy one a complete inspection and found a smaller lump on the rear of the other leg as well. She was so wooly, the lumps could not be detected except by feeling carefully. We took her to the University of Minnesota School of Veterinary Medicine for diagnosis. They believed it was caught early enough that chemotherapy treatment was worth trying — our choice, of course. We opted to try it and after three treatments the tumors in her lymph nodes had shrunk. After the full eight weeks of treatment, she was pronounced to be "in remission."

It was October and we were all feeling really good about our decision, and with having the little one in good shape and in great spirits. She was indeed her old self again. It's amazing how much closer the bond can become after getting your pet back from death's door. Shortly thereafter, Amy had her high school senior picture taken with Muffy.

It's not that I was pessimistic, but I dug a grave anyway that fall, and covered the hole and dirt pile with straw, just in case. Without a pre-dug grave, had she died during the winter in Minnesota, she might have been in the freezer until spring unless I could thaw the ground. At that point in our lives we were not big on cremation, another option for a pet lost in winter. Later, Amy would give me the business for digging the hole early, saying I had no faith. It turned out to be a good decision.

Muffy had a great winter, as she just loved the snow. Everything seemed to be going fine. But her passion was digging in the hayfields for mice, so spring was her time. On the first really warm spring day in early April, when almost all of the snow was gone and the top few inches of ground were starting to thaw, she went out and dug for hours. The next day she was down flat as a pancake and had no strength whatsoever. A trip to the U animal hospital confirmed the cancer had returned and the prognosis was terminal. They put her on a steroid for comfort and it was then up to us to measure how she was doing. We came up with a simple plan. Muffy had good days and bad days, mostly good days at the beginning. But when she started having more bad days than good days, we all agreed we had to give her what she needed, *death with dignity*.

Rob was in graduate school in Seattle, so Amy, Laurie and I all came to the same decision on the same day, when Muffy started her third bad day in a row. We called our family vet, Dr. Steve, who offered to come to the house. We had Muffy on a towel in the living room when Dr. Steve came in. He is such a good vet that our animals are always glad to see him. In his office his style is to just talk to the pet, stroke it, give it a treat and when the critter is totally at ease, give the rabies shot or whatever. For the most part, the dog or cat seems to have little idea what is going on.

So when Dr. Steve arrived, Muffy surprisingly sat up part way. But once he came over to her she went right back down on the towel, with those so very sad eyes that had been looking back at us for the past two days. He knew it was time, but he looked around the room at each of us, one at a time. "Amy, is this what you want to do?" "Laurie?" "Bill?" We all nodded "yes" as the tears streamed down our faces.

We all said our goodbyes and he then described what would happen. The first shot would just knock her out and she would feel just fine. The second shot would stop her heart. He did his work and in a minute she was gone. Dr. Steve just quietly let himself out, and we all said our last goodbyes.

I then took her outside, wrapped in the towel, and walked to the pre-dug grave in the tree line. I set her down, removed the towel and placed her in the grave. The warm weather had only taken a few inches of the frost off the top so it was a good thing I had the hole ready to go. A week earlier I had taken the straw out of the hole and off of the dirt pile to allow it to thaw. I was able to find enough thawed dirt to get her well covered. In another week there was more thawed dirt and I finished the job. A large red quartz rock marks her place in the tree line of our old farm.

I came in from outside, stayed in the basement and cried like a baby for what seemed like a half hour. Laurie and Amy were upstairs on the phone to the kids' mom, and then to Rob, giving them the news. Apparently both of them asked the same thing: who was making all the noise? Amy just said, "Oh, that's Dad, crying in the basement."

To us, this was a good death. For those of you who have never considered putting a pet down at home, it was just the best experience ever for us in one of these situations.

People ask how we can get kitty after kitty, and puppy after puppy, when it is so hard on us to lose them? Our answer goes something like this: the sorrow of our loss, which at the time can be all-consuming, can never be so bad as to even begin to outweigh the years of joy and love our pets bring to our lives. We also believe, perhaps too proudly, that we are just about as good a home as a pet could find. It seems like a mission we have, caring for animals, as they then end up caring for us.

This just seems to be one of God's perfect plans.

On the exact opposite end of the spectrum from Muffy was the death our very special first golden retriever, Kirby. He was the second of three dogs to be lost to cancer. To this day, I can start crying when I think about how awful his death was and how we felt so helpless. This was also a terrible lesson in how *not* to manage cancer treatments in dogs. Our experience with Kirby was so crushing that when his beloved companion golden, Katie, also contracted cancer, the same lymphosarcoma as Muffy and Kirby, we hesitated doing anything but take her home. But fortunately for Katie, we did not let the memory of Kirby ruin her chances, and given the U's position that we caught it early, the subsequent chemo treatments added 26 good months to Katie's life.

You see, it was not the cancer that killed Kirby, but the treatment itself, and his death was something you would not wish on your worst enemy. Unlike Muffy and Katie, Kirby showed no external signs of lymphatic cancer, and being such a large and healthy dog, it took a long time for him to become sick. By the time we got him to the U after Dr. Steve's referral, he was into Stage 4, with the cancer attacking other organs. If we had to do all over again, we would have taken him straight home, gotten him on some comforting steroid and just made the decision when it had to be made, perhaps just a very few weeks or even days down the road.

But our experience with Muffy seemed so positive, adding about six good months to her life, so we tried cancer treatments with Kirby. Of course, Stage 4 cancers require very aggressive drugs, and we were warned that one of the drugs could actually be fatal. I'm not sure it really sunk in what that meant, but after two weeks of weaker drugs, Kirby got his first dose of the strongest drug at week three. We were told to watch him closely and to bring him in just as soon as we noticed him go down, because that was a sure sign of a bad reaction to this drug. It would happen in about 48 hours if it was going to happen.

Sure enough, after a Wednesday chemo treatment, Friday afternoon he went down like a rock. We immediately took him to the U, only to encounter a skeleton weekend staff that had no oncologist, no one familiar with his case and, we think, mostly vet school students on staff. We asked those attending Kirby to call his oncologist and tell her that he had a terrible reaction to his week-3 chemo drug. They tried to reach her and finally did, but we were not a party to the call. They came back from the call and started treating him with an antibiotic, as though he had some infection. A week later we learned from the oncologist that there was really nothing to try; Kirby was dying from the drug, and he should have been put down. She had no explanation as to why they started the antibiotic.

The oncologist never came in to see Kirby and it never occurred to the weekend staff that **Kirby was reacting so badly to the chemo drug that he was dying a very painful death right before their eyes, and ours.** How this terrible miscommunication between the weekend staff and the oncologist happened, we never did find out to any level of satisfaction. He would lie in his cage at the hospital with deep reddish brown, almost black, diarrhea. It was totally lost on the weekend staff that this cancer drug, designed to run around the body and attack areas of fast growing cells, had "mistaken" Kirby's large intestine for cancer.

Not all that unusual, actually, when you consider that the colon is continually shedding cells and growing new ones, at a very fast rate, all its life.

So there was Kirby, lying on a towel, his bowel being eaten away and oozing out, in what had to have been terrible pain and suffering, as the staff pumped him full of antibiotics to fight some non-existent infection.

This is so very hard to relive as I write this. I'm crying again. We are confident that had his primary oncologist had a chance to look at him, we would have had him put down immediately. Instead, he lived almost another 30 hours at the hands of, we assume, well meaning but ill-informed staff. Every time we came back down to the hospital, we would get the same story . . . "We're still waiting for the antibiotics to 'kick in.'" Kirby died alone in what was probably great pain.

It wasn't until we asked for a conference with his oncologist the following week that we realized the full extent of this nightmare. She was very apologetic, but we were absolutely destroyed with guilt and sorrow.

This horrible experience led to two rules we now operate under when it comes to cancer and our dogs. After Kirby died we got Bailey, and after Katie died we got Nikka. We are just so much wiser now than we were then, and we feel much more confident about what to do if either of our current cuties contracts cancer. You might find what follows of some benefit.

Rule #1. Have a very honest talk with your oncologist. If the cancer is well advanced, consider just taking the dog home and doing no cancer treatment at all. Make your special furry friend as comfortable as you can, perhaps with steroids, and then have the courage to make the right decision when it's time.

Rule #2. If you decide to treat your dog for cancer, **when scheduling the chemo treatments, accept only a Monday or Tuesday treatment schedule, never anything later in the week.** If your dog is going to have a serious, even fatal, reaction to a cancer drug, you want only "A-Squad" medical people, which would include your primary oncologist, examining your beloved pet and advising you. Had we done this, Kirby could have been seen by his primary oncologist, who would have recognized immediately what was happening, and we would have put him down right then and there, saving him many hours of suffering.

We were so completely sad and beaten by what Kirby had gone through that we did not get out of bed for two days. We would just lie there, watching old movies, reading, not saying much of anything, with Katie at our feet. We had to do barn chores and feed Katie and the cats, but that was about it. The phone would ring and we couldn't talk, just cry. We'd hand the phone to the one who was in the best control at the moment.

I've lost both parents and my great friend of 55 years, DJ. My brother died long ago in 1969, tragically. But I have never cried so hard in my life as when Kirby died. He was so special for so many reasons, and especially because he was the first dog Laurie and I had together. If the Bors ever writes a pet book, it will probably be about Kirby, or perhaps Pokay.

For Kirby, it was *how he died* that was so hard to take.

This was not dying with dignity and compassion, and to this day we are still sad about it.

As you will find out, Mitten, like Muffy, died with dignity.

Note: I must say something about the University of Minnesota Vet Hospital. It is a first class institution, where we have treated three dogs with cancer. We have also brought horses to the large-animal unit. Our experience with Kirby does not detract from all of the great work this place does, in research as well as practice.

Bailey and the blade

Puppies can get into more trouble than
maybe any critter in God's grand kingdom.

All puppy owners have their own stories, as do we. This episode
with baby Bailey is one of our favorites, and we are still thankful
for the happy ending. Bailey could not have been more than three
months old when Rob drove back from Seattle with a good friend
on a "road trip" to Minnesota. Rob lived and worked in Seattle
and earned his *Master of Fine Arts, Writing*, from the University of
Washington ("Udub"). The boys arrived, and in short order they
dumped their gear in Rob's room. We had floor mats set up for
"Fox" to sleep on, and soon their gear was everywhere.

We committed a technical error however, failing to tell the
boys that, with the new puppy on board, they should keep the

bedroom door closed at all times, lest they risk substantial damage to their shoes and who knows what else. After the first night, the boys were off to the Twin Cities to see some of Rob's old pals and haunts near Augsburg College. The door to Rob's room was left ajar and that's all little Bailey needed. He snuck in, grabbed Fox's travel kit, what Dad and the United States Army called a "shaving kit," and dragged it out into the living room. It had been left in an open suitcase, unzipped, so it was easy pickins for the little fellow.

At the time, Laurie was in Washington state visiting her sister and family in Gig Harbor, so she missed most of the fun. I came in from barn chores and found the travel kit in the living room, everything taken out of it, and Fox's plastic eye drops bottle punctured and empty. "I trust those eye drops tasted good, young man." He stared back with a "huh?"

As I sifted through the wreckage I found a razor, completely shredded, with blue, white and clear plastic bits everywhere. As I dug further, there it was, the shiny razor blade assembly, lying on the carpet, a multi-blade deal, with *two* blades. The question was, of course, *did it have a third blade that Bailey might have eaten?*

This was the only razor in Fox's bag so I had nothing to compare it to; the destroyed razor traveled alone. When the boys came home I asked Fox the rather obtuse question, "Fox, how many small blades in your razor blade assembly, two or three?" He could not recall. We noted the brand and I immediately drove to our closest big store, a Target, and found the razor. Ooops. *Three* blades!

I went home and called Dr. Steve, asking if I could bring the furry little butt-head in for an X-ray. He said sure, but there was nothing to do but to see if Bailey would pass it. Stomach surgery is serious business and is really only used in emergencies or probable life-threatening situations. Given the size of the blade, he thought it would pass, but I had to *check every stool until it did.*

Oh, perfect.

So for four days I watched Bailey like a hawk, picked up every turd (which we do anyway, but not every day), and took each one into the house to the laundry tubs, for what I called "puppy poop surgery." Four days and maybe nine or ten poops later, nothing, no blade. Puppy poop is bad stuff. Gimme horse poop or even cattle poop over puppy poop, any day.

The Bors came home from her trip and I immediately gave her the assignment of being the head puppy poop surgeon from then on. She balked . . . something about it happened on my "watch" so it was still my responsibility. My retort was swift and to the point; "He's *your* puppy. You need to help on this one." * (see note)

Two more days went by and still no blade, and I was getting a little worried since I just knew it was still inside the little grunt. At one point he came in from a poop and before Bors could start the poopy blade search, Bailey barfed up a huge grass ball. Laurie searched it and, sure enough, *there was the blade!* Uff Da, what a relief.

Apparently dogs must instinctively know that if something is upsetting or irritating their tummy, a good diet of grass can serve to envelop the menace, or perhaps cause them to barf.

Smart fellow, this little Bailey. He's now 9 years old and is such a fine gentleman. Except when he eats horse apples and then breathes on you in bed.

* Author's note: Bors and I rotate early dog bonding, training and obedience school. She works with the "boys" and I work with the "girls."

The dog who loves cats

Dogs and cats can easily co-exist in the same home.
They generally figure out who needs space
and who can be wrestled with.

Pokay just never liked the dogs and to this day she is apt to swat one on the nose if they get too close. How bad can life be for a cat of her age if you have dogs around to swat on the nose, and you can *still do the swat.*

Two of our current cats, Naoz and Scouty, always liked Bailey and Nikka, and "mixed play" was not unusual when these stray cats first arrived. But it takes two, and if you don't have a willing yet gentle dog, the mixed play either doesn't happen or can sometimes get out of hand.

Bailey gets along fine with our cats, but Nikkapup is the dog who really loves cats. Named after Annika Sorenstam, the golfer, our latest golden retriever, "Nikka" (or "Nikkapup," "Neek-o" or "Nick-L") is over five years old, but still a puppy in many ways. I think she is just perpetually young. She really likes to play with Naoz and Scouty, and they really like her. Sometimes one of these two cats will wander into the bedroom while Nikka and Bailey are on the bed with us. We will look at Nikkapup and ask: "Is that your kitty?" She may then jump down and start playing with the cat. If the cat's mood is right, we'll have this wrestling match going, with each animal knowing the rules and the limits. After all, a 65-lb. dog and a small cat could spell trouble if it goes too far. With Nikka, it never does.

Scouty Pants returns the favor outside. The dogs will be coming back with Laurie from the horse barn and Scouty will lie in the yard, low, with her ears flat, waiting to pounce. Mind you, she is a really pretty calico with bold markings, trying to act "stealthy" in a green lawn. Obviously, the dogs know exactly where she is.

But there Scouty waits, and when Nikka is close, BOING! — Scouty springs at Nikka's ears, butt or tail. If Nikka wants to play, she might just give Miss Pants a little head butt, roll her over, and start sniffing and licking the cat's guts. OK, then, mini-fight!

Our latest cat addition, Earl Gray, also loves the puppies, and will wrestle with Nikka. He also does the ambush thing outside, and as a gray tabby, at least he blends in a little. In December of 2006 we were caring for a golden retriever puppy, Baxter, from Hearing and Service Dogs of Minnesota. This was a month-long deal and, at nine weeks old, Baxter arrived and fit in right away. He would roll around with Earl Kitty on a regular basis. Baxter knew not to be rough with his baby needle teeth, and Earl did not use claws.

Pretty cute stuff.

Asthma and allergies

I wonder how many millions of people have been
denied a chance to have their cat or dog of a lifetime
because of asthma or allergies.

W hile Buttons was still around, and Mom's eyes were not itching or watering at all, we actually added two more pets, a
white rat and a cocker puppy. The white rat was my contribution. After a sixth grade science experiment with two rats, one on
a good diet and one on a junk food diet (although the term "junk
food" was not yet in use), the rats needed homes. My teacher said
the first two students to bring a note from home approving a rat
adoption would get a rat.

The white rats were female and the class named one Marilyn
Monroe and the other Grace Kelly because they were both
blondes. I was pleasantly floored when Mom said, "Oh, all right,"

and we got Grace Kelly, who shortly became "Moudy." She was my responsibility, and cleaning her cage was no treat. Still, she was such a riot to have around that it was worth it.

Little Grace was not my only white rat. Over 40 years later, in 1996, Amy came home from college with a white lab rat, Captain Elvis. It seems he was going to be disposed of and Amy's boyfriend wanted to save him, or more to the point, he wanted the Bors and me to save him. So they brought him home in a cage, and just like that, we had a white rat. Unlike Grace Kelly, Elvis was big and his messes were big, so he could never be out unless you held him or watched him closely. But he wasn't cuddly and was somewhat aloof, never wanting to stay with you. Frankly, he was a bum pet.

After about a year, he developed an infection in his foot, small at first, but one day it ballooned into one huge purple mass. That was pretty much it and I put Elvis out of his misery with one swing of a shovel. Turns out the kids were not all that upset.

Rule 29: Unless it's a dog or a cat, never accept animals from college. If you can't keep the animal, at least you have half a chance of placing a dog or a cat in a good home. No one wants a large white rat with a purple foot, except perhaps someone with a pet python or boa constrictor.

About the same time we got Grace Kelly, my aunt, uncle and cousins moved to town, and the two dads hatched a plan to get cocker spaniel puppies for the two families. Again, Mom did not object much at all, as I recall. So strange, I thought at the time, and again now. Was Mom just being a trooper, or was she just tired of swimming upstream?

It was 1956 and Dad, ever the good Republican, named ours "Ike," while my cousins' family named theirs "Mike." For a while, things went fine, and the puppy, cat and rat would actually all play together. Moudy was especially entertaining as she would sleep in my pocket or run from one person to the other across an outstretched arm. Jon, Maggie and I would take turns "stealing" her from each other by putting out an arm and coaxing her over . . . "Tranner Moudy," meaning "Transfer mouse!"

Alas, neither of the new pet additions lasted very long. Moudy committed the ultimate sin. It was not unusual for her to be out of her cage, moving about the house under a watchful eye, but not for long stretches since she would do her business anywhere. One day, someone had her out and she sort of escaped, went upstairs, got on Dad's bed and proceeded to crawl under the pillow of the bed, which had been freshly made by Mom. The rather nice and, I'm sure, expensive bedspread was folded under the pillow and then back out and around the top of the pillow, making a barrier for Moudy. No matter; she went under the pillow, hit the barrier and chewed right through the bedspread, continued under the pillow and out the back side. Problem solved.

Mom went wild and I had to find a new home for little Moudy. Boo. We kids were pretty bummed.

As our lousy puppy luck would have it, it wasn't too much longer before Mom's eyes began to itch and water, and her nose began to run. I prayed it was hay fever and it would go away, but she got worse. Mom just couldn't have Ike the puppy around. I gotta give her credit for trying, but it just wasn't in the cards. This time when we had to find a new home for Ike, we all pretty much understood. Ike was my last dog until Kirby, 32 years later. CJ and Muffy were the kids' pups and their mom's, so they were only ours on the weekends.

Here's a little secret: over the years *I have developed a cat allergy.* On many occasions, while Mitten was doing his "ear nursing," my eyes would start watering and itching. Laurie would tell me to push him away, but I just couldn't. He was my little dude. Same thing if he was just lying on my chest purring, my eyes would eventually go a little crazy, but it didn't matter. I would just endure it. Today, it's actually worse. It only takes a few minutes of being close to three of our five cats to set me off. No matter. I just suffer along, and then wash my hands and face after the bout.

Allergies to dogs and cats have denied millions the joys we have known, and it may happen right in our own family. Daughter Amy, having completed her Ob/Gyn residency in Santa Clara, California, met a fine young man, Nader, a lawyer-type. Once they became an item, she dragged him back to Minnesota several times, including a trip to our great State Fair on Labor Day weekend, 2006. He passed all of our "tests," and puts up with our family craziness. They were married in June of 2008, a grand event. Nader is a solid fellow and we couldn't be happier.

One downside — Nader is allergic to cats and mildly allergic to dogs. On the State Fair weekend we were in the middle of caring for two extra goldens, Syd and Jack. We had all four pups professionally washed and groomed to reduce the impact of the dogs on Nader's eyes and nose. We can't do much about the cats except keep them out of Nader's room and do a little grooming to keep their shedding down. Actually, Nader can pet a cat or a dog, but he must then wash his hands immediately before doing anything else. I guess the good news is that he can be in the same room as any of our cats and survive.

Now, how all of this will work out long term, who knows? Amertile loves dogs and cats, and, in fact, had two cats in California. No more . . . they have gone to live on a farm in the valley because of Nader's allergies. Actually, these weren't the greatest pets anyway, being littermates of a feral mother who must have taught them early that humans were not to be trusted. Even Amy could never catch one of them, and when guests came to visit, it was as if she had no cats at all; they would just hide and never come out. In any event, Amy's decision to give these little wild ones away can be boiled down to three things: Nader's eyes and nose.

Which prompted this question: How is a lifelong pet lover going to make a life with someone who has pet allergies? What the hay, why bother being young and in love if there aren't a few hurdles?

Quite surprisingly, they now have a yellow lab named Sasha. A shedding golden would probably never have worked, but Sasha's short coat and Nader's nose are working out fine together.

Rob and Molly have a somewhat different but related challenge. Both young writers, each was a *Loft Literary Center* mentorship winner, and each has had short stories published in very respected literary journals. Am I sounding too proud?

Anyway, besides her passion for writing, Molly is a hospital technician who is studying for her nursing certification. Rob teaches writing at *The Loft* in Minneapolis. If they could make a living writing, I'm guessing that's what they would both probably do. Our young Bohemians, for sure.

They have a small, older bungalow in the Longfellow area of Minneapolis and would love to have a cat. In fact, Scouty first found them. But Molly's father has severe cat allergies, so a cat is out. They have discussed getting a rescue dog when the time is right.

It's too bad really, when I think of all those millions who cannot have a pet because of allergies. Then again, there's always a chance a cat might turn out to be a first class "Mitten," and not everyone could cope with that challenge. Allergies, then, could be the perfect Mitten preventative.

Certainly one person couldn't cope with a "Mitten" . . . whoever kicked him out, letting the little gremlin wander around Bors' apartment building in 1981. Whoever you are, I am forever in your debt.

Now here's something you may not know: dogs can have severe allergies. What a perverse reversal. Both Bailey and Nikka have had full allergy testing, and we are now administering allergy shots to both dogs. It started with Bailey, who would go swimming at our island retreat in Northern Minnesota, and in spite of having his fur blow-dried, would still break out the next day in weeping sores on his tummy. These were bad episodes. They looked so painful and he just kept licking them. A full round of allergy tests showed him to be allergic to, among other things, mice and pine pollen. Oh, perfect . . . the island is full of both. After over a year of serum inoculations and a steroid pill the day before we go to the island, and one each day at the island, he has been doing very well.

More recently, Nikka also started getting weeping sores. Nikka's battery of tests showed her to be allergic to quite a few things like pine pollen, but also including, get this, *cats*. Now both have their own special serum and each gets steroids whenever we go to the island. There seems to be a connection between getting their fur wet and their allergic breakouts, but they just have to swim at the island.

They're golden retrievers, after all.

We say goodbye

You know the day is coming to say goodbye to your four-legged
friend. Your job is to recognize that this is the day,
and then just do what needs to be done, as hard as it may be.

M itten was always a scrawny little guy with a modest appetite,
but in the fall of 2000 he just seemed less interested in his cat
food, and even kitty treats. I sprang into action and started shift-
ing him to human food.

It's not that he wasn't getting good cat food. We have always
paid extra attention to what we feed our pets, and get what we
think is the best stuff available, and age appropriate. We like to
think this has had something to do with the longevity of our cats,
especially Mitten and Pokay.

Remember my dairy product rituals with Pokay? Another
interesting story is that of our first little golden retriever girl, Katie,

and what happened after she finished many weeks of chemo at the U. of M. vet hospital for lymphatic cancer, the same cancer that struck both Muffy and Kirby. During her chemo treatments, Katie had a low white cell count from time to time. The hospital was very careful to withhold her treatment and send her home if her white count did not measure up. Given the long drive to the hospital and the sometimes wasted trip, we began having our local vet draw blood and do the white count test. If the white cell count was low, we would phone the vet hospital and tell them we weren't coming that week.

Katie's 12-week chemo schedule, which included a drug-related crisis that took her appetite (the drug was Vincristine), lasted nearly 20 weeks from start to finish. The crisis occurred after the last round of this drug. She came home and would not eat, and even stopped drinking. The next trip was to the U vet hospital's ICU. They got her re-hydrated intravenously, but food was still of no interest to her, not even hot dogs and cheese. They told us we might as well take her home and try different foods, anything just so she would eat. Katie not eating cheese? . . . she *must* be sick. We tried everything in the fridge, even warmed up stuff. Nothing interested her. If we couldn't find something soon that she would eat, of course, she would die.

I went to the Marine General Store and bought some boneless, skinless chicken breasts. I cooked them up, let them cool a bit, cut one up into small pieces, took it downstairs to the "puppy room" and sat down beside her. She sniffed the first piece, looked at it, looked up at me, sniffed again, and then took it, chewed it a bit and swallowed. Her sad little eyes looked at me again, either because she wanted more, or she was wondering why I was acting like a blubbering baby. With tears streaming down my face I sat there for maybe seven or eight minutes, slowly feeding her chicken and nothing else. After she turned up her nose at a piece, I said, "OK, little one, how about some water?" I filled a small bowl and put it next to her. She leaned over and drank some. Perfect, I thought . . . food followed by water. She went over to her round bed to lie down. She looked tired so I left the room.

An hour later I went downstairs with my tub of chicken in hand, she was awake, and we did it all over again . . . this time perhaps five minutes of slow hand feeding, followed by a little water. This went on every hour to an hour and a half, until the end of the day. The next morning Laurie tried Katie's regular dog food on her . . . no thank you, Ma'am. I then came down with the trusty Tupperware container of chicken, sat down right next to her, and did the hand-feeding thing again. Again it worked, followed again by water.

After this round I took her outside, without baby Bailey. We went out alone to avoid the little guy's enthusiasm. She peed but no poop. Bailey, our little male golden pup, came after Kirby, and he had finally stolen Katie's heart after a standoffish beginning. The older-dog-with-new-puppy thing sometimes takes a little time, but it will usually work out just fine.

After two days of hand feeding, followed by water, then a trip outside, she finally pooped and we could at last breathe a huge sigh of relief. In a couple of days I was sprinkling the chicken on top of her regular food, and she eventually started eating her own stuff after she finished the top-dress of chicken. After a week, we didn't need any chicken at all.

With a continuing drug regimen of prednisone and a mild chemo maintenance pill, Katie had another 26 months of good life, eventually succumbing to lung cancer. One day, while traveling north to our cabin, she became short of breath. We detoured to the town veterinarian in Moose Lake, Minnesota. She was put on oxygen and X-rayed, which showed her lungs full of cancer. We put her down immediately. She is buried with Kirby's ashes at our island retreat in northern Minnesota, a place they both loved surely as much as our farms.

Pokay, of course, is our ultimate success story of human food helping to keep a pet going, her dairy-product treats lasting these many years. Katie was more of a human-food-as-jump-start success. Tubby met an early grave, but I doubt a lack of appetite would have been a problem for this guy, even in old age. He was the cat that chewed through sheet rock to get at a sack of cat food.

The human food thing failed little Mitten. His last weeks were typical, I suppose: less of an appetite, losing stool control, not wanting to do much but sleep, maybe extra crying for no apparent reason, no interest in grooming, and weight loss. As the smallish Amy would say, Mitten was never over eight lbs. "soaping wet." He was barely five lbs. when he died.

I could not find a human food he would eat except for an occasional piece of cheese, and even then he would eat only two or three small pieces.

In the end he was telling us it was time, getting weaker and weaker. Dr. Steve had no particular diagnosis, except old age. One night it just seemed it would be his last. He was so very weak but after we lifted him up on the bed, he managed to curl up between Laurie and me, and spent the night with us. He purred a bit, then went to sleep, never moving. In the morning he was even weaker, and could not walk or even stand. We put a towel in a cardboard box, got the car warm, called Dr. Steve and took him straight in. Mitten got his usual "It's the relic!" comment from the vet. We laughed, then cried. We said our goodbyes and in a minute or two, he was gone.

We buried him in the pine grove of the new farm. The new house wasn't done yet and we were still living at the old farm a half mile away, but there was no question . . . we were *not* going to bury him in a place we knew we were going to leave.

It was December but the ground was not yet frozen under the heavy mat of long, tan Norway Pine needles. It was really amazing how peaceful the whole thing was. There were tears, of course, but no hard sobbing. It's as though it all happened just as it should.

Since then, Mitten has been joined by Bors' little barn scaredy-cat, Mokie. Callie, Naoz, Scouty Pants and Earl Gray are all young, so we don't think about losing any of them any time soon. Our miracle cat, Pokay, could go at any time given her age. Our cat cemetery will just continue to grow.

Tubby was left behind, resting in the south tree line of our first farm, alongside Muffy. When we moved, Amy was concerned about leaving the two of them behind, especially Muffy. I had to tell Amy that we would not transplant the decaying bodies — it was their resting place — but rather, I would take a scoop of earth from each gravesite, and if taken deep enough, ought to have at least a few molecules of Muffy and Tubby. Those two scoops of soil are also in the pine grove of our current farm. Of course it was just a symbolic thing, and Amy approved.

A good death, death with dignity, is what a pet deserves as its days become numbered. Making a beloved companion hang on to life because the human owner cannot tolerate the loss is perhaps understandable, but very wrong.

Mitten died with dignity.

Life after death . . .
The Rainbow Bridge

Being good Minnesota Swedish Lutherans (ok, I'm only half Swedish but the Bors is made of 100% lutefisk), we believe in the life hereafter. For many who believe as we do and who've had beloved pets, I'm sure the notion of pets living beyond this life has been a question. We look in their eyes, sense how much they love us, how gentle they can be, how they know when we are upset or sick, it all just seems to lead us to the same conclusion: they have souls and there is a heaven for our furry friends. We bury them or spread their ashes at their special places, and say a prayer, just like we would any family member.

Our only question was this: Is their heaven the same as our heaven? You know, do we get to see them again?

Losing Kirby sent us into a world of grief that, thankfully, did not last too long. Something that helped was a little story called *The Rainbow Bridge*. It was sent to us by a wonderful friend, Shari, written in her own hand, and came with no attribution.

For those who still grieve for a lost pet, grab some tissues.

The Rainbow Bridge

There is a place connecting Heaven and Earth. It is called the Rainbow Bridge because of its many colors. Just this side of the Rainbow Bridge there is a land of meadows, hills, valleys and forests, filled with green grasses and singing birds. When your beloved companion animal dies, this is where they go.

There is always tasty food and cool water, and warm Spring breezes. The old and frail are young again; the maimed are made whole again. They play all day with each other and all seems right, except there is one thing missing. They are not with their special family members who loved and cared for them on Earth.

They run and play until the day comes when one of them suddenly stops playing and looks up. The nose twitches, the ears are alert, the eyes are staring and they suddenly run from the group. You have been seen and when you and your special friend meet, you take them in your arms and embrace them so tightly. Your face is nuzzled again and again . . . and again . . . and you look once more into the beautiful eyes of your trusting friend.

And then you wipe the tears of joy from your eyes, turn and cross the Rainbow Bridge together . . . never again to be separated.

· · · · ·

We have tried to find out who authored *The Rainbow Bridge*, but our research was inconclusive. Whoever wrote it deserves the gratitude of many.

Perhaps you will want to share *The Rainbow Bridge* with someone special who has lost a beloved companion, or just go back and read it yourself when it is your turn to grieve.

If you're looking for Biblical evidence that we share heaven with animals, try *The Bible Answer Book* by Hank Hanegraaf, starting on page 135.

Dad and Buttons have long since been re-united. Mitten is playing near the Rainbow Bridge now, waiting for me.

I'm not exactly sure how the shared pets work, like Muffy, Kirby and Katie. *The Rainbow Bridge* might suggest that the first one of us humans who gets there takes all the shared pets across, and they will then all wait across the bridge for the rest. I suspect the shared ones continues to wait for the human it was the closest to.

I guess for the shared ones, we'll just have to see.

I'll croak first, of course. Statistically, the Bors will outlive me by 30 years, a notion that has led to some mild friction. She talks about adjacent urn plots or ashes being spread at the same place, and I counter with something like . . . "Hell, you'll be on your third husband by age 80, and you'll outlive him as well as me and number two. You're too young and healthy to be planning this stuff with me." She just gives me a "grrr."

Pokay might greet me, but she will continue to wait for her beloved "mom," the Bors.

I recently had a chance to send *The Rainbow Bridge* back to Shari. A rat coming home from college is not a good thing, but cats are another story. When Rob was in college he found a dorm stray, which he tried to keep but the Resident Assistant said it had to go. He brought Otis home and we made a video, which I took to work, along with a little poster. The marketing of Oti had begun.

Shari came into my office and asked about the cat. I handed her the video and said, "If he looks good on tape, you can try him out, but if he doesn't work out, we'll take him back. We had him vet-checked, he's had all his shots and he was already neutered."

Oti was with Shari and her family for 14 years and just recently passed away. I hope she appreciated *The Rainbow Bridge* as much as we did when she sent it to us after Kirby died.

Mitten again?

If the world wasn't ready for the first Mitten,
how will it ever handle another?

To close this book, I was going to offer that a *new* Mitten had wandered into our lives, Little Miss Scouty Pants. She's smart, funny, gets into everything, is quite independent, and at times can be a total pain in the ass. She is especially a pest to our other cats. She's the first cat since Buttons to climb the Christmas tree, but so far hasn't matched Button's stunt of tipping the whole thing over. Scouty even nurses on me, right on the beard whiskers. Agony! A great early resumé, don't you think?

Son Rob took immediate exception to the comparison. "All superficial stuff," he said. "Scouty loves everyone . . . Mitten only loved *you*." Not quite the truth because the little guy had a great affection for the Bors as well. But I have to admit that Rob was partially right. It was perhaps Mitten's grouchiness (Amy called him "Mr. Grumpy Pants") that set him apart from all the other pets we've ever had. He may have been a grump to many, but I never really noticed. My love for the little wiener was blind.

What Rob has not seen, however, is a relatively new side of Scouty. If she doesn't like what you're doing, she'll give you a little chomp. *Very Mitten-like.* She also does that sort of love-hate thing . . . the purring bite, something the kids have not seen since the Mitten. She really is more like the Mitten with each passing day. What a riot.

Amy's memory produced this little gem. Having the two orange tabbies, Tubby being so easy-going and Mitten being the grump, the kids came up with this rhyme to keep them straight: "Nose is yellow, gentle fellow. Nose is white, he might bite." Of course, Tubby's nose was orange like the rest of him, not yellow, but then, orange doesn't rhyme . . . with anything, I guess.

I think they fashioned this after the "Which snake is it?" diddy that is used to tell the poisonous coral snake from the king snake . . . "red on yellow, kill a fellow". . . or is it black on yellow? Good thing I live in Minnesota and not Arizona.

There really can't be pet replacements, anyway, can there? You lose a special pet and you want another. By the way, we *never* bought into that crap about waiting a decent mourning period before going out and finding another. There were always plenty of cats and we never felt any of them needed to be replaced any-way . . . it all just happened by itself with the cats.

But when we lost Kirby, feeling just so awful and sad, we were out there almost right away looking for another litter of goldens.

Mourning period . . . schmourning period! This is when we found Nancy, our current golden breeder. We think she's just a very sound breeder, and we will stick with her for as long as she stays with it. She gave us Bailey after we lost Kirby, and then Nikka after we lost Katie. Our pattern seems to be a male golden followed by a female maybe two to four years later, so that we always have a "bridge" dog. I have no idea how we would have survived losing Kirby without having Katie around. Then, adding little Bailey soon after Kirby's death was just the best medicine ever for us and, eventually, for Katie as well.

The enrichment of our lives by these wonderful critters has been beyond measure. While many of our friends talk about this being their last pet so they aren't tied down and can travel without the hassle of figuring out what to do with the dog or whatever, we could not imagine our lives without our beloved little four-leggers.

When the next pet shows up, you notice the differences immediately. There they are, being themselves, not replacing at all, just being new and unique, to be loved and to love you.

Perhaps after reading this book you might become a first time pet owner. If you have been a dog person all your life and now think you can't handle a dog, consider a cat.

You might even find a "Mitten" of your own, a true *cat of a lifetime.*

Epilogue

How does a cat get to age 24? Get to 23 and then refuse to die.

It seemed appropriate to write something special for Pokay, given everything she has been through. One hilarious episode happened just before Christmas 2006, and is just the typical Pokay-quietly-cheats-death-again story. Mitten dodged his bullets in yarns worthy of the great storytellers. With Pokay it was usually much more subtle, where I just shook my head and said . . . "Well, she's still with us." The exception, of course, was her stay in the neighbor's garage at Johnson Lake, which was, according to Amy, drama of the highest order.

By December 20, 2006, our holiday guests had arrived, at least those who were staying for a few days. From Seattle came sister Meg and husband Dan, then Amertile arrived from California. All three are cat fanciers and were excited that we now had *four* full-time house cats, Earl being the latest to graduate from the barn to the house. Caring for two extra hounds added to the commotion. Bailey and Nikka had to share quarters with "Baxter," a 9-week-old golden pup we were taking care of for Hearing and Service Dogs of Minnesota. We also had the 90 lb. (and still growing) Bernese, Walter, who was only 10 months old, still pretty much a puppy. Walter only stayed a week, but the golden stayed a month. Neither of these new guys had been around cats so it was a bit of a challenge at first, but it eventually worked itself out.

What chaos.

I got up the morning of the 21st and found cat barf in maybe six different places around the house, places where Pokay hangs out. Some of it was pink, indicating it contained blood. Pokay was moving very slowly, with her back arched, as though her stomach was really hurting. She just seemed so sad.

Expecting the worse and remembering Kirby, we did not want to prolong her suffering, so we called Dr. Steve and made an appointment to see him right away. We said we thought it was "her time." His office is only eight minutes away.

When we got there Dr. Steve was in the back, so his assistant asked us whether we wanted to take her back home today or have her cremated. The frozen ground might have made burial difficult, but we said we would take her home. If we couldn't dig a hole due to frozen ground, she might just have to stay in the big freezer until we could build a fire and thaw the ground. She said the euthanasia fee was $39, but we could pay it later. I gave her $40, got a buck back with a receipt, and we waited for Dr. Steve.

Pokay, ever the mystery cat, was now *purring*. In fact, she started purring in the car as we approached the vet's office, and by now she was in full roar. Hmmm?

Dr. Steve came into the front room and asked that we put her down on the floor. We did and she immediately walked to the next room, purring away. We were so embarrassed yet so elated. "They don't generally move around much and purr when it's their time to go. Tell me more about her symptoms." As we shared what we knew, he asked, "OK, how much did she eat yesterday?" It was at that point that Bors and I compared notes and realized the little beggar had buffaloed us individually into really overfeeding her the day before. She paid the price that night by walking around the house, losing everything.

Dr. Steve went on to say that frequent vomiting can cause minor bleeding, and that it was probably because of the vomiting that her tummy was now so sore that she was walking with an arch in her back. *"It's **not** her time."* Yes, we felt embarrassed, but totally overjoyed.

He listened to her heart and it was fast. He was concerned about thyroid problems, given her good appetite but continuing weight loss. He took some blood for lab analysis and we took Pokay home.

As we walked in the door our holiday guests were expecting a dead cat, ready for burial or the freezer, and a bunch of tears. Instead, we set our purring Pokay down and she went about her business. They all started to howl. "Pokay!" OK, false alarm.

She's now on two new drugs and is doing great. You go, little Po. Pokay is still with us and is doing just fine, thank you, so my idea of ending the book with a tribute to a departed Pokay, her epitaph so to speak, just isn't happening, which is grand indeed. Editor Pat says it could start my next book. *Next book?* Uff da!

Hold it. She's in the kitchen meowing for dairy products right now. "I'm coming, Pokay. I'm coming."

. . . . .

Nearly one year later . . .

How exactly does a book of this kind get finished? Over the past year I've added some stuff, come up with some ideas about pictures, and editor Pat has been through this end-to-end. Here it is Tuesday, December 4, 2007, and I'm still fooling around with this thing. I'm under orders from Pat to get the pictures rounded up so we can at least say we have everything. We now have maybe 50 or so potential photos, most of them pre-digital. We'll need to trim this down a bit.

So, as the book remains unfinished, new things can be added, right? Up until we actually close it off, some things good, and some not so good, can still go in.

Today at 4:05 p.m. little Pokay's soul flew to the Rainbow Bridge at the age of 23 years 10 months and 2 days. She collapsed last Friday, November 30, of what looked like a stroke. She could not get up. For the second time in just under a year, Pokay went to Dr. Steve's with the notion of putting her down, only to have her come home again, still breathin'. This time he thought we should try liquid potassium to see if perhaps she suffered muscle failure due to a potassium shortage. She has been on potassium pills, ground up and mixed with cream, but about a week ago she stopped eating it, so his liquid potassium idea sounded plausible.

She came home for the equivalent of kitty nursing home care, which turned out to be more like kitty hospice. We made her comfortable in a dog kennel in our room, allowed her to lie on a diaper, and we served her liquid food, liquid potassium and, of course, all the liquid dairy products she would eat. Dr. Steve said if the potassium was the issue we would know in about two days, with Pokay trying to stand again. It never happened.

Yesterday she stopped taking liquid food; she would only take cream. She was getting weaker and wasting away by the hour it seemed.

As mentioned earlier, winter burials can be a challenge in Minnesota. This has been a very cold fall, November being especially frigid. Saturday I tested the ground in the pet cemetery in the pine woods and it was rock hard. I started a fire in a fire ring, let it burn down to coals, and in two hours the ground was thawed. I dug the hole, saved the dirt in two 5 gallon pails and placed them in the basement so the soil wouldn't freeze. I then covered the hole so it wouldn't fill with snow. Good thing . . . in two snowfalls just after my digging, we got over 11 inches of snow.

It took very little time at Dr. Steve's. We said our goodbyes, cried quietly . . . and she was gone. We took her home and laid her to rest. Just like Mitten, it seemed to happen just as it should. A wonderful life, a quiet death with dignity, tears but no sobbing for the Bors and me. Earlier in the day I made her headstone to match those of Mitten and Mokie. Pretty easy to do since we have some cement stone cut into triangles left over from the new house construction. Some black magic marker for her name is all it took. After the snow stopped, the Bors placed the headstone on Pokay's grave.

I still say her name from time to time after she's gone, just not as often as the Mitten. Losing my cat of a lifetime was followed seven years later by the Bors losing hers.

The Rainbow Bridge is waiting, and God has surely provided plenty of room for additional furry souls. We will lose more of our little friends before it's our turn.

At the bridge I will have hugs and kisses for all who have gone before, but my biggest hugs will be for Kirby and Mitten.

In time, I will find Jon.

Final resting place for Mokie, Pokay and Mitten